Easy Beans

Easy Beans

SIMPLE, SATISFYING RECIPES THAT ARE GOOD FOR YOU, YOUR WALLET, AND THE PLANET

JACKIE FREEMAN

Photography by Angie Norwood Browne

SASQUATCH BOOKS

SEATTLE

Contents

Introduction

You have an interest in beans, have you? Step into my kitchen, grab a plate, and let me show you a thing or two. . . .

First things first: Who am I and what can I tell you about beans? In addition to feeling that I'm constantly losing my beans, both figuratively (I'm very busy) and literally (we have a large pantry), I'm a professional chef with over twenty years' experience in the food industry. I have slogged my way through restaurant and catering kitchens; honed my skills as a private chef, food stylist, and recipe developer; and was even a goat midwife and cheese maker (another story, for another time). I'm also a busy wife, mom, and auntie with a mind toward time and budget and the ever-present challenge of feeding the hordes before hangry sets in.

But about beans. I think we can agree they need better PR. Oftentimes they are seen as boring, flavorless, and difficult to cook. A health fad of genera-tions past or something to eat only if you are avoiding animal protein. Nothing, however, could be further from the truth. Beans are a powerhouse of nutrition and are naturally available in a convenient (and quite pretty) little package. They come in a variety of colors, flavors, textures, and sizes, and are used in recipes from all over the world. You can start with them fresh, dried, frozen, or canned and transform them into any number of dishes.

Current food trends are leaning toward more mindful eating: healthy for the body, healthy for the wallet, and healthy for the planet. Cooking with beans is a natural choice. They're a highly nutritious and budget-conscious plant-based protein that works for both meat and nonmeat eaters alike. Best of all, beans can be found at the corner stop-and-shop, the neighborhood farmers market, the mega warehouse emporium, or online as you shop from the comfort of your pajamas. Cheap, nutritious, and appealing to every palate—who could ask for more?

My goal here is to offer you forty-two delicious bean-centric recipes perfect for everyday meals. From breakfast (including—yes!—smoothies) to snacks to salads to mains, these recipes show that beans are no ordinary or forgettable kitchen staple.

Beans in a Nutshell . . . Rather, a Podshell

In a nutshell—rather, a podshell—a legume is any plant whose seed is enclosed within a pod. Beans are the seeds from those different plants (though we normally refer to the whole kit and caboodle as a *bean*). And pulses are the dried, edible seeds of a legume plant. Still don't have your finger on the pulse, literally or metaphorically? Unlike legumes that are harvested fresh (think fresh beans, fresh peas, soybeans, and even peanuts), pulses are harvested dry once they have fully matured on the plant. Pulses have a long shelf life, making them a perfect pantry staple, compared to a fresh-harvested legume that should be eaten or frozen within a few days. All beans are legumes, but not all legumes are beans. So green beans aren't really beans; they're actually legumes (because you eat the fruit in the pod), and black-eyed peas are really beans despite their name, and peanuts aren't nuts but are actually legumes (a seed that grows in a pod underground), and alfalfa is a legume, though we rarely eat it (unless you happen to be a horse).

FRESH, DRIED, AND CANNED

There are so many beans available today, at specialty stores, run-of-the-mill grocery stores, and online markets, that choosing which to cook with can be overwhelming. Fresh? Canned? Dried? Frozen? Heirloom? No matter what you choose, there are some basic rules to live by:

Fresh or Frozen

If you're lucky enough to grow beans in your garden, there is nothing quite like eating a freshly picked shelling bean for flavor and texture (plus they cook up really quick!). If it's not the right season or you lack a green thumb, fresh beans can sometimes be found in your supermarket. Don't overlook frozen beans: raw edamame and lima beans, once cooked, are wonderful thrown into stir-fries, salads, and pasta dishes.

Canned

Canned beans are perfect for quick soups, salads, and entrées, and offer a wide variety with little to no planning required (no need to soak or cook them). Look for beans that don't have added sugars, salt, or other additives (like sodium metabisulphite or calcium chloride). Canned beans are about twice as expensive per serving as dried beans, but if time is your priority, then it might be worth the cost, at least occasionally. Always rinse and drain your canned beans before adding them to your dishes to get rid of that murky water (except in the case of aquafaba; see page 93). Canned beans can be stored in your cupboard like any other canned food. If you live in a particularly damp climate or are extremely clumsy with your cans, you might want to consider writing the name of the bean somewhere on the can in case the label comes off, so you're not playing Russ-bean roulette.

Dried

Dried beans are inexpensive to buy and can be stored for months to years without spoiling. And with a little forethought, they are easy to prepare and taste better than canned beans. Learn how to sort (see page 16) and soak them (see page 19) before cooking (see page 23). Dried beans can be purchased in small packages or bulk from most grocery stores and corner markets. Transfer them to clean, airtight containers (I like glass canning jars so I can admire their beauty and easily see what I have and how much) in a cool, dry place. As beans age, they need longer soaking and cooking times, so it's wise to use them within one year for the best flavor and texture.

Keeping Cooked Beans

Whether you have leftovers by accident (they do double in size after cooking and are quite filling) or on purpose (you decided to make a double batch to save time later), cooked beans can be refrigerated for up to 5 days. Or transfer them to serving-size sealable plastic bags and freeze for up to 6 months. When you need some cooked beans to toss into a soup or salad, they are at your fingertips.

TO YOUR HEALTH: WHY BEANS ARE GOOD FOR US, OUR WALLETS, AND THE PLANET

Research has shown that eating a few cups of beans a week as part of a healthy diet can help you lose weight and prevent heart disease, type 2 diabetes, and even certain types of cancer. The same oligosaccharides that give you the toots are also a form of prebiotics, a food source that promotes healthy gut bacteria. (Read more about how to avoid the dreaded bean toots on page 12.)

Different types of beans have different health benefits, but in general all beans are high in dietary fiber, a good source of low-fat plant protein, low in sugar, and low in sodium. They all provide B vitamins and folate; minerals like potassium, magnesium, manganese, copper, iron, zinc, and phosphorus; and antioxidants. Beans are a powerhouse of healthy food in a perfect little package.

Let's dive a little deeper into the nitty-gritty, healthy-wealthy:

Protein

No matter if you are a pro athlete or a couch surfer, everybody needs protein in their diet. It helps to build, grow, and repair our bones, muscles, enzymes, and tissues. It's also been shown to fight off viruses and bacteria (there's nothing like a bowl of Bubbe's homemade chicken noodle soup to help fight a cold). Beans provide one of the highest levels of plant protein available.

However, beans are not entirely perfect. Protein is made of amino acids. While meat, fish, dairy, and eggs can provide all twenty-one amino acids essential for human life, beans lack one of them: methionine. But don't despair! When paired with grains, beans form a complete protein with all twenty-one amino acids present and available, especially important for those on a vegetarian or vegan diet. Most of the time, you don't even have to think about pairing beans and grains—many cultures all over the world have been doing it for centuries: Mexican beans and rice or tortillas, Middle Eastern lentils and rice, Indian dal and naan, British beans on toast, Italian bean soup with a slice of focaccia, even hummus (which is a combination of chickpeas and tahini, which is made of sesame seeds that provide that missing amino acid).

Beans and grains don't necessarily need to be eaten together at the same meal to reap the benefits of forming complete proteins. You can technically eat a dish of beans for lunch and a bowl of grains for dinner with the same benefit as eating them together at breakfast. But since they taste so good together, why not?

Fiber

Fiber helps you feel satiated when you are eating and long after you are done with your meal. Beans are low on the glycemic index, meaning their form of carbohydrates has a steady rise and a steady fall in our blood glucose levels, versus sugary carbohydrates (like cookies), which give us peaks and valleys, causing us to feel hungry more quickly. Beans provide two types of fiber: soluble and insoluble. Insoluble fiber (think roughage) helps to keep you regular. Soluble fiber helps to keep blood sugar and insulin levels on an even keel, reducing the risk of type 2 diabetes and lowering LDL ("bad") cholesterol.

Cholesterol

Many of us, especially as we age, need to watch our cholesterol levels. While meat and dairy often have high levels of saturated fat and cholesterol, beans are low in fat (most of that fat being unsaturated) and are cholesterol-free.

Other Health Benefits

Though protein, fiber, and cholesterol are all important, we need more than that to be healthy. Beans are a great source of calcium, magnesium, and phosphorus (which build strong bones and teeth) and have high levels of potassium, which is helpful in lowering blood pressure and improving kidney function. They are packed with zinc, which is especially helpful in boosting the immune system during the cold and flu season (who can resist a warm pot of bean stew on a cold night), and are a good source of B vitamins and antioxidants.

Healthy for the Planet

It takes less energy (in the form of land use, fertilizers, pesticides, machinery, antibiotics, and water) to grow plants than it does to raise livestock. Plus, as indigenous people discovered long ago, using legumes in crop rotation (and growing them alongside corn and squash) actually enriches the soil. They are nitrogen fixers, meaning they pull nitrogen from the air and deposit it into the soil, requiring less chemical fertilizers than other crops. Pound for pound, beans can feed more people than animal products, while using less energy.

Healthy for Your Wallet

Cooking with beans can also reduce your grocery bill. Instead of buying cheap food that's low in quality or low in health benefits, buy healthy food that is cheap: beans. If you're a meat eater, cutting out animal protein a few times a week and swapping it with beans will make a big difference in the billing department. You can spend that extra money on higher-quality cuts of meat when you do buy it for dinner. Of course, the cheapest beans are the dried variety, but even canned beans can be cost effective.

"BEANS, BEANS, THE MAGICAL FRUIT": BEANS, GAS, AND YOU

It's time to talk about the (gassy) elephant in the room. . . .

Ask any kid under the age of ten about beans, and you're most likely going to get a raucous rendition of the infamous lyric "Beans, beans, the magical fruit, the more you eat, the more you toot. The more you toot, the better you feel, so let's have beans for every meal." There is some fallacy in this rhyme, foremost that beans are not fruit but legumes. But the rest? Pretty darn accurate. All of that fiber does have, er, consequences, but a happy digestive system leads to a happy person.

So what can you do to reduce gas?

Beans contain carbohydrates called oligosaccharides that can't be processed by our digestive system. The oligosaccharides pass through our upper intestine and then are fermented in our lower intestine. Like a great batch of sauerkraut or kimchi, this fermentation produces a certain amount of gas, which then must pass one way or another.

But fear (or fart) not! There are several ways that you can reduce or eliminate awkward moments after a meal. The first is by pacing yourself. If beans are new in your diet, slowly add them to your meals over several weeks or months. Let your body get used to this new form of carbohydrate.

Some suggest that soaking your beans anywhere from four to twelve hours ("overnight") will help leach out some of the gas-producing bad boys. And if you are thinking of soaking your beans to begin with . . . you're already ahead of the game!

Cooking your legumes so that they are intact, but soft and creamy on the inside, will also help to reduce gas. An undercooked bean is more likely to lead to a loud disturbance later on than a fully cooked bean.

Many cultures around the world have discovered that adding a few key herbs and spices greatly helps to reduce windy repercussions later on. An added bonus? They also make the beans taste great. Add a piece of dried kombu (a type of seaweed) to your Japanese-inspired dishes; a fresh epazote leaf or ground cumin to your Mexican meals; asafetida, turmeric, or ginger to Indian curries and stews; or fennel or sage to your Mediterranean-inspired dishes.

Prebiotics

Most of us are familiar with probiotics, found in yogurt, fermented veggies, and little capsules that we always forget to take. But what the heck are prebiotics? Prebiotics are a type of dietary fiber (hello, beans!) that feeds the good bacteria in your belly. This gut bacteria then produces nutrients for your colon cells and leads to a happier, healthier you. Boiling it down: prebiotics are the food for probiotics. So beans not only feed you, they feed all those teeny-tiny superbeneficial bacteria in your gut. Win-win!

The Heat Is On: How to Properly Cook Your Beans

Is it worth the effort to cook beans from scratch? In short: yes. The long answer is that it doesn't require too much work on your end, and you will enjoy a superior flavor and texture over what you can achieve with canned beans. Of course, I'm not knocking canned beans. There is a time and place for them—and usually that time and place is a mad dash to get dinner on the table.

Before we get too deep, a few notes on cooking beans:

- Stove-top cooking should always be done at a simmer.
- Instant Pot and pressure cooker times are based on low pressure with a natural release of ten minutes.
- In a slow cooker, most of the time it will take six to eight hours on low.

All cooking-time suggestions in the following recipes are just that . . . suggestions. Start checking your beans for doneness at the beginning of the time frame, but know that it might take much (much, much) longer depending on how old your beans are and what they've been through physically and emotionally before they landed in your cooking vessel. Also, everyone's cooking vessel is different. What might take nine minutes on high pressure in one pressure cooker may take eight minutes at low pressure in another. One person's medium-high heat on their gas stove is different from another's medium-high heat on their electric burner. So test, test, test (to test for doneness, see page 25).

OUT OF SORTS: HOW AND WHY TO SORT YOUR BEANS

Most beans that you buy in bulk have been sorted, but it's always a good idea to give them a rinse and look them over for the errant pebble, stick, bandage, or added protein (bug). Trust me, it happens.

Simply place your beans on a large rimmed (so they don't fall off) baking sheet and take a quick peek for broken or irregular pieces, small debris, or anything else you don't want to add to your meal.

Helpful Conversions

1 pound dried beans = 2 cups dried beans = 4 to 6 cups cooked beans

1 cup dried beans = 2 to 3 cups cooked beans

1 (16-ounce) can beans = 1½ cups drained beans

1 cup dried lentils = 2½ cups cooked lentils

You may notice that many recipes call for 1½ cups cooked beans (or a multiple thereof). That's no coincidence. Pop open a can and go for it!

BEAN BATH TIME: HOW TO SOAK BEANS

There has been some debate of late about whether beans need to be soaked before cooking. Some people vote that you must always soak your beans to make them tender and help reduce the toots (see page 12). Others believe that they'll cook up just fine and soaking beans leaches valuable nutrients. Who's correct? Both. Neither. Who knows?

Here are my two cents: some legumes benefit from a good soaking (think tougher varieties, like chickpeas and pinto beans). Some legumes don't need a bath (think softer varieties, like lentils and black-eyed peas). The rest? Like life, it's totally up to you. (Check out the Bean-cyclopedia on page 151 for suggested soaking, or not soaking, times.) Also, like all other food, the fresher beans are, the better they taste (and the easier they cook). Yes, you can keep a bag of beans tucked away in your cupboard for a year (or two, or gawd, probably longer), but the quality will suffer. The fresher the bean, the less soaking (if any) it needs. But how are you to know if that bag you picked up at the grocery store has been hanging around for one day or one year? You don't. So probably best to err on the side of caution.

The Quick Soak

Despite its name, the quick soak is not entirely all that quick, in the sense that it requires some work from you. Place your beans in a large pot and cover them with plenty of water. Bring the water to a boil, remove the pot from the heat, and let the beans soak for one hour. Drain the cooking liquid and start cooking your beans as called for in your recipe.

The Long Soak

This method requires a little more forethought, but less work. Simply place your beans in a large, nonreactive (glass or ceramic) bowl, and cover with at least double the volume of water. Let soak, uncovered, in the refrigerator for four to twelve hours. Then drain, rinse, and cook. At this point, you may want to leap into the future and read about salt and brining your beans for maximum flavor on page 20. But don't forget to come back now, y'all!

How to Know If Beans Are Soaked Enough

It's always a good idea to check to see if your beans have been properly soaked. Cut one bean open—if it is an even color, the water has fully penetrated the bean. If there is an opaque spot, you need to either soak them a bit longer or add a few minutes of cooking time.

Lentils and split peas do not need to be soaked before cooking. Simply place them in a sieve, rinse with cool water, drain, and then add them to your recipe. Easy, peasy, pulse-y.

TO SALT OR NOT TO SALT, THAT IS THE QUESTION

This is the question that has divided nations and families and led to some really angry grandmothers. To salt or not salt your beans, and when, where, and how?

Anecdotal evidence suggests that adding salt to the pot will result in tough skins and longer cooking times. Scientific evidence (I'm looking at you, Harold McGee) suggests otherwise. So what should you do? In general, I belong to the camp that salts toward the end of any type of cooking. I want my food to absorb flavor from the ingredients in the pot (whether it be a handful of herbs, flavorful stock, a few chopped veggies, or a slab of bacon), and see where it lands when almost done. So I may add a pinch (okay . . . a generous pinch) of salt to the cooking water. But I would rather undersalt my food at the start of cooking and reseason it at the end once I know what the final dish is going to taste like, than risk oversalting from the beginning.

That being said, I also believe in the power of a good brine to add depth of flavor to food. And you can actually brine your beans, just like turkey, chicken, and pork. If you're choosing to soak your beans (see page 19), try adding one tablespoon kosher salt for every one quart water. Give it a good stir and let your beans hang out in this slightly salty mixture when they soak. After soaking your beans, always drain and rinse them really well so that you don't add too much salt to your pot.

Let's talk about "salt to taste" when seasoning your recipes. You'll notice that all of the recipes encourage you to salt to your taste. Why is that? Because tastes vary . . . a lot. After some very scientific* research, it appears that my "salt to taste" for the average pot of beans is one-half to one teaspoon. My friend Jill, whose experience lies between advanced home chef and novice professional, is one-eighth of a teaspoon. My mom, who tries to avoid salt at any cost, is a single grain from the saltshaker. Where do you land? The only way to find out is to add salt to the dish, then taste it! And if you're feeling like things are a bit humdrum, add a little bit more.

NO-NOs?

Avoid adding acids (likes tomatoes or vinegar) or sugars (like molasses or brown sugar) early on in the bean-cooking process, as these toughen cell walls and keep the beans from softening. And despite what your grandmother may have taught you, do not add baking soda to your cooking beans. The skins may soften more quickly, but there is also a good chance they will taste like soap (and lose nutritional value to boot). Of course, I suggest you add baking soda to The Only Hummus You'll Ever Need (page 47), so who am I to talk?

No scientists were harmed in the undertaking of these experiments.

HOW TO COOK BEANS

A sturdy, large old-fashioned pot with a lid is really all you need to cook your next meal. However, our kitchens nowadays are filled with all of the latest gizmos and gadgets to make our lives easier. You can use your stove top, pressure cooker or Instant Pot, oven, and slow cooker to cook beans, but keep a few things in mind:

Stove Top

Place your beans in a large pot. Add just enough water or stock to cover by one inch and bring to a boil. Boil for five to ten minutes, and then reduce the heat to a simmer. Cover and keep simmering until your beans are intact but tender. This can range from thirty minutes to three hours, depending on the type of bean you are using and how old they are. Gently stir the beans and check the liquid level every so often to make sure they are not sticking or getting parched.

Pressure Cooker and Instant Pot

While pressure cookers and Instant Pots greatly reduce cooking times, they are not really instant, and you run the risk of a pile of mush. It will take about ten minutes for the pressure to build, then the programmed cooking time, then another ten to twenty minutes to depressurize the pot. I suggest reducing the cooking time so the beans are *almost* cooked through. You can select

Edamame
Many of these recipes call for "cooked" edamame. Most of the time, edamame is kept in the freezer section of the grocery store, along with frozen veggies. To cook, it's as simple as following the directions on the bag, usually boiling in heavily salted water for 3 to 5 minutes, and then draining. For the least amount of work, buy shelled edamame so you don't have to remove the pods.

low pressure, do a quick or ten-minute natural release, or finish the process with the lid off so you can monitor the beans closely. Leave plenty of room for the beans to cook—they will froth up and expand a lot (up to three times their original size). So never fill the cooker more than one-third full, unless you want to spend all evening scrubbing your countertops. If you have an older pressure cooker (one with a jiggle top), watch that the vent doesn't become clogged (it will make a loud hissing noise). If it does, immediately and carefully remove the cooker from the heat and release the pressure.

Oven

Baked beans are both a dish and a way of life. When baking beans low and slow in the oven, you can (1) oftentimes skip the soaking step, and (2) experience fewer burst beans because they are simmered so gently. Place your beans in an oven-safe pot with a lid (hello, Dutch oven!) and cover them with water, making sure to give them enough space to expand (up to three times their original volume). Preheat the oven to between 275 and 325 degrees F, bring the beans to a boil on the stove top, cover, then transfer to the oven. Then simply set it and forget it, cooking the beans until tender (forty minutes to three hours, depending on the bean). But, of course, don't actually forget them. . . . Give a check and a stir every once in a while to see how they are progressing and if you need to add more liquid.

Slow Cooker

When using a slow cooker, you still need to soak your beans beforehand (if that's the route you normally take). And it's a good idea to bring them up to a boil for a few minutes before cooking long and slow. Because it's hard to tell when the beans are done, check after the first five hours, then every thirty to forty-five minutes after that.

Checking for Doneness

How will you know when the beans are done? Carefully hold a bean in between your fingertips and give it a squeeze. If it collapses into a creamy mass, it is ready. If it's a bit mealy or firm, keep cooking for a little while longer and check again. Also, you know, you could always taste one.

Though I mention cooking times in the Bean-cylopedia at the back of the book (see page 151), those times can vary a lot depending on the age of your beans, local humidity, and, quite frankly, luck. Start with the lower end of the cooking times and check for doneness.

In an Instant

What's the difference between a pressure cooker and an Instant Pot? The newest gadget to hit the market, the Instant Pot is a multicooker. It does all the same work as a pressure cooker but will also steam rice, make yogurt, slow cook, sauté, and babysit your children. Use whichever you have on hand, no judgment (except for babysitting the children . . . maybe).

An Important Note about Lima Beans and Kidney Beans

Lima beans and kidney beans do require some extra care to eat safely. The lima bean family contains small, natural levels of cyanide, so always cook lima beans, whether they are dried or fresh. All kidney beans contain a toxin called phytohemagglutinin, but red kidney beans contain the highest levels. The best way to ensure you don't get a stomachache (or worse) when cooking dried kidney beans? Soak them overnight, change the water, and bring them to a boil for a full 10 minutes, which deactivates the toxin.

Starts + Smoothies

RECIPES FOR BREAKFAST

———

They say breakfast is the most important meal of the day. Of course, I have no idea who this "they" is or what authority "they" have. All I know is that if I don't have breakfast every day, and usually first thing, there is hell to pay. And a bowl of cereal or a croissant will not cut it for me. I need a healthy balance of carbs, fats, and proteins. An actual balanced meal. Otherwise I crash, and I crash hard. Just ask any of my unfortunate family members who happen to be around me a few hours after I've woken and not had breakfast (so sorry, y'all!).

Most of us have reached for a doughnut or cold pizza slice while running out the door in the morning. Is it the best breakfast choice? Probably not. Does it sometimes happen? It certainly does. And I bet we can all admit that even though the sugar or carb rush feels great in the moment, we all crash physically and mentally soon after (perhaps requiring us to reach for another doughnut or cold pizza slice—it's a vicious cycle).

Do you know what have a healthy balance of carbs, fat, and protein? You guessed it. . . . And do you know what are easy to prepare (especially if you have them frozen from previous meals or canned on the shelf), great tasting, and superversatile? Yep, you're on a roll now. . . . Let's get started, then.

HOW TO: SMOOTHIES

Okay, don't roll your eyes at me or flip to a different chapter in the book just yet. . . . Stay a moment. Beans. Smoothies. Beans and smoothies. Yes. And here's why.

Most of us have made (and loved) a smoothie for breakfast or a postworkout snack. They are quick and easy to make, portable, require no utensils to eat (aside from a straw, perhaps), and are filling, versatile, and delicious. Also, most of us pack our smoothies with healthy ingredients to get the most bang for our buck nutrition-wise: nut butters, different types of milk, grains, hemp or chia seeds, vegetables, protein powder, just to name a few.

You know what else is a superhealthy ingredient, packed with protein and fiber, and low in fat? What adds creaminess to a dish and will keep you full for hours? Yep.

I don't want to keep you from whipping up a smoothie and trying it out, so here are a few facts to help get you on board:

If you read up on the health benefits of beans (see page 7), you'll know that they are packed with fiber. When you start your day with a full serving of fiber, you start your day feeling full. Which means less snacking and better food choices for hours afterward.

You can save both time and money in the morning making a five-minute meal. Next time you cook up a large batch of dried beans (see page 6), set some aside and place them in small portions in your freezer. You can actually mix all your main smoothie ingredients (beans, fruits, and veggies) in small containers and freeze them. Then, when you're running out the door, grab a preportioned mixture, add a little liquid of choice, and whip them together in your blender. Bam. Breakfast.

Keep in mind that not all blenders are created equal. If you're lucky enough to have a top-of-the-line blender, (1) congratulations, and (2) can we be friends? Just toss everything in willy-nilly and blend. If you have a, um, lesser-quality blender (author raises her hand), add the liquid first, then the frozen items. Start blending on low speed and work your way up to high speed.

In this chapter, I share with you some of my favorite combinations, but this is a great time to experiment. Follow the recipe to a *T* or mix in whatever beans you happen to have on hand. Mix and match different leftover beans with different fruits and veggies. One of the wonders of beans is that they can be easily blended into different dishes.

Now that you are on board with bean smoothies (see, I told you!), what if you have too much of a good thing? If you have more smoothie than you can drink, keep the leftovers in the refrigerator for up to a day. Better yet, freeze the leftovers and make Popsicle smoothies to replace late-night ice cream feeding frenzies. Healthy and satisfying. You're welcome.

V Recipes marked with this symbol are vegan friendly!

Chocolate, Banana, and Black Bean Smoothie Ⓥ

Is it breakfast or dessert? You decide.

MAKES 1 SERVING

1 cup almond milk
1 cup packed fresh spinach
½ cup cooked black beans (or substitute navy beans in a pinch)
1 medium frozen banana, cut into chunks

1 to 2 pitted Medjool dates, roughly chopped
1 tablespoon cocoa powder
Pinch of ground cinnamon (optional)

In a blender, combine the almond milk, spinach, beans, banana, dates, cocoa powder, and cinnamon. Puree until smooth.

Tropical White Bean Smoothie

Warm tropical beaches, the sound of a gently lapping ocean, carpool with the kids.

MAKES 1 SERVING

1 cup plain kefir
½ cup cooked cannellini, navy, or great northern beans
½ cup frozen mango chunks

½ cup frozen pineapple chunks
1 small banana, broken into pieces
Honey

In a blender, combine the kefir, beans, mango, pineapple, banana, and honey to taste. Puree until smooth.

PB&J Smoothie Ⓥ

I am a lover of PB&J sandwiches. I had them for school lunch almost every day growing up. I also had them for dinner almost every evening growing up. (If we didn't like what my mom had prepared, we were obligated to take one bite, then make our own dinner. PB&J was simple and tasty.) And now, as a busy mom, I make them for breakfast at an alarmingly high rate. They are fast, easy, and fit the bill of healthy (protein and whole grains) and filling (again, protein and whole grains). But sometimes I want to mix it up a bit. Don't get me wrong, though. I don't want to stray too far from my perfect-sandwich comfort zone. Thus, enter stage left: this smoothie is all the best things about a PB&J sandwich, in drinkable form.

MAKES 1 SERVING

1 cup frozen strawberries

1 cup oat milk

½ cup cooked chickpeas, great northern, or cannellini beans

2 to 3 tablespoons peanut or almond butter

1 tablespoon chia seeds (optional)

In a blender, combine the strawberries, oat milk, chickpeas, peanut butter, and chia seeds. Puree until smooth.

Lentil and Oat Granola ⓥ
with Coconut and Almonds

I love a bowl of granola in the morning. Okay, I also love a bowl of granola for lunch, dinner, and a midnight snack. Topped with yogurt or milk (or ice cream). This version is packed with protein and fiber and will definitely fuel you for the day ahead or satisfy your cravings at night. Plus, it's also vegan and gluten-free, if that's your jam. If that's not important, it's darn delicious and you can feel pretty good about yourself anyway.

Cook the lentils a little shorter than normal so they are just al dente (a little *tooth* to them) and drain completely. Otherwise you'll have a sloppy mess on your hands when you go to bake them with the oats and nuts.

MAKES ABOUT 1 QUART

2 cups cooked red or yellow lentils (or a combination), cooked al dente

1½ cups rolled (old-fashioned) oats

1 cup raw sliced almonds

1 cup unsweetened coconut flakes

¾ teaspoon ground cardamom

Big pinch of kosher salt

½ cup maple syrup

¼ cup melted coconut or canola oil

½ teaspoon vanilla extract

Preheat the oven to 325 degrees F. Line a baking sheet with parchment paper.

In a large bowl, combine the lentils, oats, almonds, coconut, cardamom, and salt. In a small bowl, combine the syrup, oil, and vanilla. Drizzle the oil mixture over the lentil mixture, and toss well to combine so that the dry ingredients are evenly moistened.

(CONTINUED)

Spread the granola on the prepared baking sheet and gently press into an even layer. Bake for 50 to 60 minutes, until golden and dry to the touch, rotating the pan occasionally so it bakes evenly. Remove from the oven and let cool completely before breaking into clusters.

Store in an airtight container at room temperature for up to one week.

Swap it out: If you're not a fan of cardamom, or don't normally keep it in your cupboard, cinnamon is a great substitute.

Granola Is Endlessly Variable

You can add different nuts and seeds while cooking, or dried fruit and even cocoa nibs after the granola is cooked and completely cooled. Or keep it simple and use only lentils and oats, but top it off with fresh fruit right before serving.

Xoi Dau Den ⓥ
(Vietnamese Black Bean Sticky Rice)

Traditionally, this dish would be cooked in a banana leaf in a conical bamboo steamer. But the reality is, most of us don't own such equipment or have the time and energy to care. So a plain ol' saucepan (or rice cooker or Instant Pot) will do just fine. Because you do need to soak the rice, start the prep before bedtime, then pop it on the stove to cook while you're showering, catching up on emails, brushing your teeth . . . whatever it is that you need to do in the morning.

MAKES 4 TO 6 SERVINGS

1 cup glutinous rice (also known as sweet or sticky rice)

1½ cups cooked black beans

¾ cup canned full-fat coconut milk

½ cup water

3 tablespoons granulated sugar

Pinch of kosher salt

¼ cup roasted salted peanuts

¼ cup unsweetened coconut flakes, toasted (see page 38)

2 tablespoons sesame seeds, toasted (see page 38)

Rinse the rice and soak in several inches of water (it absorbs a lot) for at least four hours and up to twelve hours, in the refrigerator. Drain and rinse.

In a medium saucepan over high heat, combine the rice, beans, coconut milk, water, sugar, and salt. Bring to a boil, stirring occasionally. Cover with a lid set slightly askew to vent, then reduce the heat to a simmer. Cook until the rice is done, about 12 minutes. (Use a fork or spoon to pull some of the rice aside. Look into the hole, and if the water is completely absorbed, turn off the heat. If there is still water in the pot, cook for another 5 minutes until the water has been absorbed.)

(CONTINUED)

Remove from the heat, cover completely, and let steam for an additional 12 minutes.

In a sealable plastic bag, mix the peanuts, coconut flakes, and sesame seeds. Smash with the back of a small frying pan, meat mallet, or metal bowl. To be really authentic, forgo the plastic bag and lightly mash it all with a mortar and pestle.

Divide the rice mixture among bowls. Top with the peanut mixture. Serve hot.

Toasting
When you toast coconut flakes, nuts, and seeds, it brings out their natural oils, which boosts their flavor. There are two basic ways to toast these goodies: oven and stove top.

Preheat your oven to 350 degrees F. Spread the coconut, nuts, or seeds on a rimmed baking sheet and toast until fragrant and just starting to turn golden. Shake the pan halfway through toasting to ensure an even toast. Generally speaking, the lighter the item, the less time it needs in the oven (coconut flakes and sesame seeds may take 2 to 5 minutes, walnuts 6 to 8 minutes, and hazelnuts 8 to 10 minutes). Follow your nose: pull the nuts and seeds just as they start to smell good. Leave them too long and they'll burn quite quickly. Immediately transfer them to a plate so they don't continue to toast (burn) on the hot baking sheet.

If quick and dirty is your way, or a cool kitchen is preferred, toast them in a dry skillet over medium-high heat, shaking the pan continuously. When you start to see a bit of brown or smell a bit of toast, immediately remove the skillet from the heat and transfer your goodies to a plate.

Cool completely and store in an airtight container for up to 1 week.

Huevos Rancheros Sandwiches

Maybe this is not a superauthentic refried bean recipe, but it's delicious, filling, and easy enough to make in the morning when you're trying to get out the door. If you find you're always in a rush to get breakfast on the table, the beans can be made a day (or two, or five) before and reheated with a touch of hot water or zapped in the microwave. If you have extra faux refried beans, tuck them away for later to layer in a burrito, scoop up with chips and salsa, or scarf down by the spoonful because you're so darn hungry and they're so darn tasty.

MAKES 4 SERVINGS

For the faux refried beans:
1½ cups cooked pinto beans, warm
½ teaspoon ground cumin
½ teaspoon dried oregano
¼ teaspoon chili powder
Splash of hot water
Kosher salt and freshly ground
    black pepper

For the sandwiches:
4 English muffins, halved and toasted
4 slices Colby jack or cheddar cheese
1 ripe avocado, pitted and sliced
¼ cup salsa
4 large eggs, cooked how you like 'em

To make the faux refried beans, in a small bowl, mash the beans, cumin, oregano, chili powder, and enough water to get your desired consistency. Season to taste with salt and pepper.

To make the sandwiches, with a heavy hand, spread the bean mixture on the bottom of each English muffin. Place a slice of cheese on the bottom halves, followed by a few slices of avocado and a dollop of salsa. Top with an egg for each sandwich and finish with the English muffin tops. Grab a lot of napkins and eat immediately.

Make it vegan: Swap out the eggs for tofu slices and leave the cheese at home.

Snacks + Spreads

RECIPES FOR NOSHING

———

I come from a long, proud line of noshers. We snack when we're tired, awake, bored, interested, distracted, working, resting, driving, hiking, visiting, drinking, watching a movie, reading a book . . . and sometimes even when we are just hungry. We snack in groups and alone. Eating is our family pastime. I even married into a family of snackers, which makes visiting the in-laws perfectly in my comfort zone. In fact, we've been known to stand around a fully cooked dinner headed toward the table, and noshed our way through the entire meal just standing there. What can I say? It's a gift.

Beans lend themselves perfectly to noshing. They are tiny, flavorful vessels willing and ready to be transformed into any variety of dish, whether it be creamy, crunchy, or somewhere blissfully in between. Packed with protein, these nibbles are equally delicious whether you're standing around the kitchen chatting with your family, impressing guests at your cocktail party, or mindlessly stuffing your face while watching reality television. But, you know, in a healthy way.

HOW TO: HUMMUS

The ubiquitous chickpea spread, hummus, can be found almost anywhere: next to a pile of pita wedges, slathered on a sandwich, or as a dressing for pasta salad. You can buy this spread at the grocery store, but what you get lacks flavor and inspiration. Make your own for less money than buying it and with many ingredients you may already have on hand. Plus, once you master the basics, this simple combination of chickpeas and tahini can become so much more. But before we jump out of our hummus comfort zone, let's learn how to make the best basic hummus possible.

1. No beans about it: The truth of the matter is, hummus is all about the beans. Unlike most recipes (and everything I tell you otherwise in this book), if you're soaking and cooking your own dried chickpeas (see page 159), cook them with a pinch or two of baking soda until they fall apart (the baking soda raises the pH of the water and helps to break down the beans into a pulp). Ditto with canned chickpeas, but cook them for just 10 minutes to make sure they are perfectly tender.

2. Top shelf: Since the ingredients in hummus are so simple, there's nothing to mask the flavor. Use fresh lemon juice (not bottled), fresh garlic (not jarred), and the best tahini you can find. If you're worried that your hummus might also ward off vampires, remove a bit of the bite by letting the garlic and lemon juice mingle for a few minutes before blending with the remaining ingredients.

3. Blended, not stirred: Now is not the time to hand mince this spread to creamy perfection. If you haven't already, invest in a food processor or blender. You'll find you can use it for innumerable kitchen tasks (including smoothies; see page 29).

The Only Hummus You'll Ever Need ⓥ

Yes, you can easily buy hummus at the grocery store, but making your own will take your taste buds to a whole new level of creamy, savory perfection. Plus, your family and friends will find it pretty darn impressive when you set out a *mezze* platter with the homemade stuff.

MAKES ABOUT 3 CUPS

1 cup dried or 2 cups cooked chickpeas
1 teaspoon baking soda
3 to 4 medium cloves garlic, peeled
Freshly squeezed juice of
   1 to 2 medium lemons
Pinch of kosher salt

⅔ cup tahini
1 to 3 tablespoons cold water,
   plus more as needed
Sprinkle of ground cumin
Extra-virgin olive oil, for drizzling

If using dried chickpeas, soak them covered by 3 to 4 inches of water using the quick or long method described on page 19. Drain and rinse. If using cooked chickpeas, drain and rinse if necessary.

Place the chickpeas and baking soda in a large saucepan. Add water to cover by 3 inches. Bring to a boil over high heat, reduce the heat to a simmer, and cook until the chickpeas fall apart, about 45 minutes for dried or 10 minutes for cooked. Drain and rinse.

In the bowl of a food processor or blender, combine the garlic, juice from one lemon, and salt to taste. Puree and let sit for 5 to 10 minutes.

Add the tahini and pulse to combine. With the motor running, add cold water 1 tablespoon at a time to create a smooth, pale paste. Add the chickpeas and process until smooth, stopping to scrape the sides as needed. Add a little bit of water to achieve the desired consistency. Season to taste with additional salt, lemon juice, and cumin.

Serve in a shallow dish with a drizzle of olive oil or store in an airtight container for up to 5 days.

Mix It Up

Now that you've perfected basic hummus, it's time to experiment.

- Switch the beans: Instead of chickpeas, try using other beans, like black-eyed peas, edamame, or black beans.
- Add fresh herbs: Make a green goddess hummus by adding a handful of fresh leafy herbs, like parsley, basil, or chives.
- Add other produce: Give a pop of color and flavor by mixing in a few slices of well-drained roasted red peppers, pitted olives, or roasted beets or carrots.
- Play with the spice: Instead of cumin, add a pinch of sumac, za'atar (see page 132), or red pepper flakes.

Open Sesame

Tahini is a paste made from ground sesame seeds. Believe it or not, those sesame seeds provide the missing amino acid necessary to turn chickpeas into a complete protein. How cool! Have too much of a good thing? Use your extra tahini in salad dressings, mix with yogurt to top roasted vegetables, add a tablespoon to soups and stews, or even use it in your baked goods!

Edamame Fritters
with Parmesan and Mint

There are so many wonderful things I can say about these fritters. They are simultaneously crispy, cheesy, bright, light, and satisfying. They are so tasty that my meat-and-potatoes husband actually took the leftovers to work, fully knowing that there was no meat or potatoes in the fritters. Now, that's really saying something. And, at the risk of sounding shallow, they are pretty good-looking all dolled up with a curl of Parmesan cheese and fresh sprig of mint.

In order for the fritters to hold together, you need to get just the right consistency of chunky and smooth when chopping the edamame. If the pieces are too large, the fritters fall apart. If chopped too fine, they're a mushy mess. Aim for pieces that resemble rice kernels, with a few pea-sized chunks thrown in. And don't be afraid to use a (lovingly) firm hand to form the fritters.

MAKES 8 SERVINGS

1½ cups shelled cooked edamame (see page 23)

1 cup dried bread crumbs, divided, plus more as needed

¼ cup (about ¾ ounce) grated Parmesan cheese

3 tablespoons chopped fresh mint

2 tablespoons minced shallot (from about ½ small shallot)

1 tablespoon finely grated lemon zest

2 medium cloves garlic, minced

2 large eggs

Kosher salt and freshly ground black pepper

Pinch of red pepper flakes (optional)

3 tablespoons high-heat oil, such as canola or safflower, for frying

(CONTINUED)

In the bowl of a food processor or blender, pulse the edamame until not-too-finely but not-too-coarsely chopped. Transfer to a mixing bowl and stir in ½ cup bread crumbs, cheese, mint, shallots, lemon zest, garlic, and eggs. Season to taste with salt, pepper, and red pepper flakes. Mix until blended.

Form into 8 patties, about ½ inch thick. Place the remaining ½ cup bread crumbs on a plate. Carefully roll the fritters in the bread crumbs to coat the outside, pressing gently as needed.

Line a plate with paper towels.

In a large sauté pan over medium heat, heat the oil. Fry the fritters until golden brown, 3 to 4 minutes per side. Drain on paper towels. Eat right away.

Make it meaty: Add a bit of diced ham or prosciutto to the mix.

About to Crumble

What's the difference between fresh and dried bread crumbs? Fresh bread crumbs are just finely crumbled bread. They are light, moist, and great as binders, but they don't hold well for extended periods. Dried bread crumbs have had a little quality time in the oven, removing extra moisture. They add a bit of crunch as well as act as a binder, and they can be kept in the cupboard for months.

Lentil and Mushroom "Caviar" Ⓥ

I'm sorry, did you say bean caviar? What. The. [Insert favorite expletive here]. Gross. No, no. Let me explain. Back in my catering days, we used to make this amazing spread-dip-topping that was chock-full of as many mushrooms and herbs as we could muster. I don't know why, but we always called it "caviar." Maybe the name comes from the mushrooms being chopped superfine, with a bit of a glisten from the vinegar, making it almost look like the real deal? Maybe it was a way to sell cheap ingredients for a high price? Maybe it just sounds nicer than "mushroom spread"? Whatever you call it, it's [insert that favorite expletive here, again] delicious. Pile it on toast points, scoop it up with endive or radicchio leaves, sprinkle it over your scrambled eggs, or just eat it with cheap crackers while standing in front of the open refrigerator door . . . doesn't matter. It's that good.

MAKES 2 CUPS

3 tablespoons extra-virgin olive oil
½ pound fresh mushrooms (wild, cultivated, or a combination), finely chopped
¼ cup minced shallot (from about 1 small shallot)
2 medium cloves garlic, minced
1 cup cooked brown lentils

2 tablespoons balsamic vinegar
Kosher salt and freshly ground black pepper
¼ cup chopped fresh leafy herbs (parsley, oregano, marjoram, or tarragon, or a combination)
1 teaspoon chopped fresh thyme

In a large, heavy-bottomed skillet over medium heat, heat the oil. Add the mushrooms and cook until they release their juices, 5 to 7 minutes.

Add the shallots and garlic and cook until fragrant, about 2 minutes. Gently fold in the lentils and vinegar and cook to warm through, about 3 minutes. Season to taste with salt and pepper.

Remove from the heat and let cool slightly; fold in the herbs. Serve warm, at room temperature, or cold. Store in an airtight container in the refrigerator for up to 5 days.

Baked Butternut Squash and Black-Eyed Pea Samosas

True confession: I love puff pastry. I use it for sweet dishes, I use it for savory dishes, I use it for dishes that are a combination of sweet and savory. I have even occasionally made it from scratch in culinary school, for work, and just for fun. But goodness, it is a lot of work. So, further confession: I really, really love store-bought frozen puff pastry. No one will ever know the difference (except for you, and you won't have to spend a lifetime—or what feels like it—making the stuff, so who cares?).

Speaking of shortcuts, you should always use fresh butternut squash for this recipe. Ha! Who are we kidding? (Sorry, still laughing about that one. . . .) If you don't have the time, patience, or season for fresh butternut squash, absolutely grab a bag of your favorite chopped squash from the freezer section. Simply thaw and drain it, and zap it in the microwave. That's what I do, and no one has ever been the wiser.

MAKES 12 SAMOSAS

2 tablespoons high-heat oil, such as canola or safflower

1 large yellow onion, diced

4 medium cloves garlic, chopped

2 teaspoons mild curry powder

1 teaspoon mustard seeds

1 teaspoon fennel seeds

1 teaspoon cumin seeds

1 teaspoon garam masala

2 tablespoons water

1½ cups cooked black-eyed peas

1 cup cooked butternut squash cubes

¼ cup chopped fresh cilantro

Kosher salt and freshly ground black pepper

1 large egg

2 sheets frozen puff pastry, thawed

Mango chutney or sour cream, for serving (optional)

(CONTINUED)

Preheat the oven to 400 degrees F.

In a medium skillet over medium-high heat, heat the oil. Add the onion and cook until softened, about 7 minutes. Stir in the garlic, curry powder, mustard, fennel, cumin, and garam masala. Cook until fragrant, 1 to 2 minutes, then deglaze (scrape up the delicious brown bits on the bottom) the pan with the water. Cook and reduce the liquid until it's a thick paste, about 2 minutes.

In a large bowl, combine the onion mixture, black-eyed peas, and squash. Gently mash, leaving about ¼-inch squash chunks, with a fork or potato masher. Fold in the cilantro and season to taste with salt and pepper. Set aside.

In a small bowl, mix the egg with a splash of water to form an egg wash. Set aside.

Line a baking sheet with parchment paper or a silicone mat. Lay a sheet of pastry on a lightly floured surface. Cut into thirds, then cut each third in half crosswise. Roll out each piece into a 5-inch square.

Working with one square at a time, use a pastry brush or your fingers to brush the edges with a little egg wash. Spoon a generous tablespoon of the filling into the center. Fold the square in half to form a triangle; pinch together the edges to seal. Place on the prepared baking sheet. Repeat with the remaining pastry and filling. Lightly brush the tops of the pastries with egg wash.

Bake until golden and puffed, 20 to 25 minutes. Serve warm with a dollop of mango chutney or sour cream.

Butter Bean and Walnut Dip

Butter bean? Why am I calling it butter bean dip instead of what it really is
. . . lima bean dip? I think we'll agree that the former has a better ring than
the latter. But you and I both know that butter beans are lima beans and lima
beans are butter beans, so let's call the whole thing off. All that being said, I
do prefer to reach for the slightly larger, paler butter beans when I whip up a
batch of this dip. But regular or baby lima beans will work just as well. You'll
find this concoction is garlicky, creamy, spreadable, and dippable, perfect
smeared onto crackers or toast points, or dipped into with fancy crudités.

MAKES ABOUT 1½ CUPS

4 medium cloves garlic, minced
Finely grated zest and freshly squeezed
   juice of 1 large lemon
1½ cups cooked butter (lima) beans
½ cup toasted walnuts, roughly chopped,
   plus more for serving (see page 38)

¼ cup (about ¾ ounce) grated
   Parmesan cheese
¼ cup extra-virgin olive oil
1 to 3 tablespoons hot water, as needed
Kosher salt and freshly ground
   black pepper
Chopped fresh parsley, for serving

In the bowl of a food processor or blender, add the garlic, lemon zest, and
juice. Let sit for 5 minutes.

Add the beans, walnuts, Parmesan, and oil. Pulse until the desired consistency
is reached, scraping down the sides of the bowl as needed. Add hot water to
thin, if necessary. Season to taste with salt and pepper.

Transfer to a cute (or not cute) bowl and garnish with the parsley.

Swap it out: Want to go even greener? Swap out the lima beans with cooked
edamame (see page 23).

Marinated Black-Eyed Peas and Olives Ⓥ

As you already know, I love snacking. What you may not know is that I especially love snacking if I can use food as a utensil. This dish sort of crosses the border between dip, spread, and snack. It's essentially a fancy tapenade. For those brave at heart and with nimble digits, pick and peck at it by scooping it up with crackers, celery sticks, or endive leaves. For those a little more discriminating or a little less dexterous, use a spoon to carefully place it on omelets or toast points topped with goat cheese, or use it to stuff roasted mushrooms.

MAKES ABOUT 2 CUPS

3 tablespoons red wine vinegar
2 tablespoons finely chopped shallot
(from about ½ small shallot)
1 medium clove garlic, minced
½ teaspoon fennel seeds
3 tablespoons extra-virgin olive oil
2 teaspoons chopped fresh thyme

2 teaspoons chopped fresh oregano
1 teaspoon chopped fresh rosemary
1½ cups cooked black-eyed peas
½ cup assorted pitted brine-cured olives, rinsed, drained, and roughly chopped
1 tablespoon finely grated orange zest
Red pepper flakes

In a small bowl, mix the vinegar, shallots, garlic, and fennel, and let sit for 5 minutes. In a separate small bowl, mix the oil, thyme, oregano, and rosemary.

In a medium glass bowl, combine the shallot mixture, herb mixture, black-eyed peas, olives, zest, and pepper flakes to taste. Cover and refrigerate for at least 1 hour, preferably overnight, stirring occasionally.

For the best flavor, bring to room temperature before serving or store in an airtight container in the refrigerator up to 5 days.

Swap it out: Don't have black-eyed peas on hand? Swap them out with cooked navy beans. Are you all out of rosemary? Use your favorite combination of herbs. Try mint, parsley, chives, and/or dill.

Greek Fava ⓥ
(Yellow Split Pea Dip)

Bet you think this dip is made with fava beans, right? Gotcha! Traditional Greek *fava* is actually a spread made with yellow split peas. This spread will thicken as it cools, so if it seems a bit runny right off the bat, relax and give the spread and yourself a few hours to chill. It's great as an appetizer served with pita bread or crudités, dolmas, Marinated Black-Eyed Peas and Olives (page 59), and a nice glass (or two) of wine—you've got a party!

MAKES ABOUT 3 CUPS

2½ cups vegetable stock or water
1 cup dried yellow split peas
½ medium red onion, chopped
3 medium cloves garlic, chopped
1 bay leaf
Kosher salt
3 tablespoons extra-virgin olive oil, plus more for serving

2 tablespoons freshly squeezed lemon juice
1 tablespoon finely grated lemon zest
Freshly ground black pepper
2 tablespoons capers, rinsed, drained, and roughly chopped
Sweet paprika, for serving

In a large saucepan over high heat, add the stock, split peas, onion, garlic, bay leaf, and a generous pinch of salt. Bring to a boil, skimming any foam that comes to the surface. Reduce the heat to a simmer and partially cover. Cook, stirring occasionally, until the split peas are tender, about 40 minutes. Remove the bay leaf.

Remove from the heat and add the olive oil, lemon juice, and zest. Using an immersion blender, blend to your desired texture: a little chunky or perfectly creamy (alternatively, let the mixture cool for about 5 minutes and carefully transfer to a food processor or blender). Season to taste with salt and pepper.

Transfer to a serving bowl, drizzle with oil, and sprinkle with capers and paprika. Or store in an airtight container in the refrigerator for up to 5 days.

Spicy Black Bean Snack Mix ⓥ

My younger brother and I went to the same college together, at the same time, in California (thanks, Mom and Dad—we owe you!). Several times a year we would load up the old Volvo station wagon and drive sixteen hours straight from home to school. The only way we survived the trip was through continual snacking (see page 44 for a brief family history). Back in those days our car snacks leaned toward the peanut-raisin-chocolate or pretzel-nuts-and-cheese-square variety. Today, my tastes have turned a bit more sophisticated.

Riffing on the traditional snack mix of crispy, crunchy, and spicy, black beans are roasted in the oven until they turn perfectly airy-crisp. They are then tossed in a mixture of spicy (but not too spicy) flavors along with some good ol' fashioned nuts (we shouldn't stray too far from the familiar, now). It's equal parts tasty, weirdly crunchily addictive, and healthy, to get you to the end of the road—or halfway there, at least, depending on how much you make and how quick you eat.

MAKES ABOUT 3 CUPS

1½ cups cooked black beans
1 cup raw cashews, roughly chopped
½ cup raw pumpkin seeds (pepitas)
2 teaspoons high-heat oil, such as canola
  or safflower

1½ teaspoons chili powder
1 teaspoon ground cumin
½ teaspoon kosher salt
Cayenne pepper

Preheat the oven to 400 degrees F. Line a rimmed baking sheet with parchment paper.

Spread the black beans out over several layers of paper towels and blot dry. Transfer to the prepared baking sheet and roast until the beans are dry and just starting to crisp, about 20 minutes.

(CONTINUED)

Remove from the oven. Add the cashews, pumpkin seeds, oil, chili powder, cumin, salt, and cayenne pepper to taste. Mix well and return to the oven. Continue to roast until the beans are crisp and the nuts are fragrant, 8 to 10 more minutes.

Remove from the oven and let the mixture cool completely. Seriously, like so cool that you left it out on the countertop for several hours, cool. Then and only then, store in an airtight container for up to 1 week.

Swap it out: If you're looking to change it up, swap out the black beans with chickpeas or kidney beans, increasing the roasting time to 50 to 60 minutes for the kidney beans. Play around with different nuts (yeah, I heard how that sounded too) or spices. Cajun seasoning is surprisingly tasty in this mix.

Soups + Stews

RECIPES TO KEEP YOU WARM

———

I could probably live on soups and stews for the rest of my life and be perfectly happy. They have the magical power of ranging from simple to complex, easy to challenging, hearty to refreshing, and cool to hot (sounds like the perfect life partner). Soups and stews also tend to be packed with flavor. Maybe it's because they require time to simmer and really contemplate life. Maybe it's because we can throw so many delicious ingredients into them without repercussions. I guess I see them as dishes where you can throw everything *and* the kitchen sink into the pot, and they almost always come out great. No room for error, lots of room for flavor. Sounds good to me.

And, of course, beans are the perfect component for soups and stews. Toss in a handful, a can-full, or a truck-full. It doesn't really matter. A little or a lot will add texture, flavor, protein, and fiber to any pot. Fun fact: you can also use beans as a thickening agent to make your soups extra creamy. Simply blend a cup or two of cooked beans with a cup or two of stock or water, mix it into the pot, and voilà! A creamy base without the actual cream.

HOW TO: CHILI

There are as many chili recipes in the world as there are snowflakes. And just like snowflakes, they are all a little bit different. But I'm guessing snowflakes don't enter chili cook-offs, so the former are a little more competitive than the latter. So be it.

Not all chilies are made the same. Some have beef; some are red; some don't have beans, believe it or not (beans are heresy in Texas chili, but, for obvious reasons, we are going to ignore this legume discrimination and continue on . . .). Spice levels can range from the mildly amusing to the requires-hospitalization, and everything in between. Chili can be meat laden or vegetarian, thick or thin, made with any number of liquids and vegetables—and it is almost always delicious.

Before we get into the nitty-gritty, I do want to take a lexical-nerd break: *chili* versus *chile* versus *chilly*. Chili is the dish that warms us on a chilly afternoon while watching sportsball. Chili is also a pepper, powder, or sauce that you put into the dish that warms us on a chilly afternoon while watching sportsball. Chile is a pepper stuffed with cheese (hello, chile relleno and chile poblano!). Chilly is being uncomfortably cold. Good? Good.

Let's get started, then:

Protein: This can range from ground beef to ground turkey to chorizo to sausage to stew meat to beans, or a combination thereof.

Liquids: You can always use water, but, though convenient and cheap, it's boring. Try beer, stock (beef, chicken, or vegetable), or tomato or vegetable juice.

Spices: The world is your oyster here. And, in addition to the common chili spices (chipotle, chili powder, smoked paprika, cumin, cayenne, and oregano), try a bit of the sweet to balance the savory (cocoa powder or cinnamon).

Vegetables: Always start with a base of onions and garlic, but try adding other veggies. Think peppers (bell, jalapeño, or poblano), corn kernels, sweet potatoes, tomatillos, or butternut squash or pumpkin. And don't forget the tomatoes. Or do forget the tomatoes. It's up to you.

The finishing touch: One of the best things about chili is customizing your bowl at the table. Offer up shredded cheese, sour cream, sliced green onions, cilantro leaves, or sliced avocado. Or serve it alongside tortilla chips or cornbread, on top of a baked potato, or with rice.

Sweet and Spicy Red Chili

I have always been a fan of chocolate—mostly in the bar or ice cream form (I would never turn down a cookie or brownie, though. . . . I'm not a monster). My first encounter adding chocolate to savory food was in my teenage years, in a chance encounter with mole. I was blown away, both by the deep, dark flavors and the concept of adding chocolate to a savory dish.

The combination of cocoa powder and molasses in this chili makes it surprisingly dark and rich. It's *almost* akin to mole, but with a heck of a lot less ingredients and a heck of a lot less work. Oh, and it's chili, not mole. So there's that too. And a friendly PSA: remember to use Dutch-process cocoa powder in this chili, not the stuff you use to make hot chocolate with a certain young lady from the Alps on the package.

If you are so bold to cook this dish outdoors in a Dutch oven over coals, you can add another s to it and make it sweet, spicy, and smoky.

MAKES 6 TO 8 SERVINGS

1 tablespoon high-heat oil, such as canola or safflower

1 pound 85 percent lean ground beef

2 medium green bell peppers, chopped

1 to 2 jalapeño peppers, finely chopped, seeds optional

1 large yellow onion, chopped

4 medium cloves garlic, minced

2 tablespoons chili powder

2 tablespoons Dutch-process cocoa powder

2 teaspoons dried oregano

¼ cup molasses

¼ cup dark brown sugar

1½ cups cooked kidney beans

1½ cups cooked pinto beans

1 (14-ounce) can crushed tomatoes

1 (16-ounce) can amber beer

Chicken stock or water, as needed

Kosher salt and freshly ground black pepper

Chopped green onions, both white and green parts, for serving

Sour cream, for serving (optional)

(CONTINUED)

In a large heavy-bottomed pot or Dutch oven over medium heat, heat the oil. Add the beef and cook, breaking it up, until just browned, about 5 minutes.

Add the bell and jalapeño peppers, onion, and garlic; cook until softened, 5 to 7 minutes. Stir in the chili powder, cocoa powder, and oregano. Add the molasses and brown sugar, and stir.

Add the kidney and pinto beans, tomatoes, beer, and enough stock to just cover, if needed. Bring to a boil, reduce the heat to a simmer, partially cover, and cook for 30 to 40 minutes to allow the flavors to meld.

Season to taste with salt and pepper. Serve sprinkled with green onions and dolloped with sour cream.

Make it vegan: Looking to go all bean or go home? Leave the beef at the door and double up on the beans.

Too Hot to Handle
Ouch! When working with hot peppers, make sure to wear gloves or wash your hands thoroughly after chopping. You don't want to get the oils from the peppers on your hands, then accidentally touch your eyes, nose, or other, um, sensitive regions.

Edamame and Arugula Soup Ⓥ

The ingredients are simple, though I admit they do sound a bit odd mixed together. But trust in the process, and you'll be delighted with the results or your money back (just kidding, you own the book already)! The preparation is easy (a tween could make this). And the result? Light and refreshing, yet somehow creamy and comforting. I was really tempted to up the garlic to four cloves so I could say something cheesy like "four ingredients times four." But it's good how it is, so the crème fraîche will have to be as close to something cheesy as you get in this one. Also, this soup really benefits from a good blitz— now is the time to whip out your superfancy blender or just keep at it until the soup is nice and creamy.

MAKES 4 TO 6 SERVINGS

1 tablespoon extra-virgin olive oil
½ medium red onion, chopped
2 medium cloves garlic, minced
4 cups shelled raw edamame (see page 23)

4 cups vegetable broth
4 cups packed baby arugula
Kosher salt and freshly ground black pepper
Crème fraîche, for serving (optional)

In a large saucepan over medium heat, heat the oil. Add the onion and cook until soft, about 5 minutes. Stir in the garlic and edamame and cook until fragrant, about 2 minutes. Pour in the broth and bring to a simmer. Cook until the edamame is tender, about 15 minutes.

Remove from the heat and stir in the arugula. Using an immersion blender, blend the soup until smooth (alternatively, let cool for about 5 minutes and carefully transfer in batches to the bowl of a food processor or blender). Season to taste with salt and pepper.

Divide between four bowls and serve with a dollop of crème fraîche.

Swap it out: Don't have crème fraîche? Don't get fraîche with me. Substitute a dollop of sour cream or plain Greek yogurt, or just eat it as is.

Turkey and White Bean Chili

Despite popular belief (well, the belief of my husband and teenage nephew, at least), not all chili needs be red. This version goes for the white-and-green look: white beans, turkey, tomatillos, green chilies, cotija cheese. It's as equally delicious as the more well-known red chili (see Sweet and Spicy Red Chili, page 71), just with a different flavor profile. I find it brighter, lighter, and slightly more healthy to eat, which of course, means I eat three times more than I probably should. Ah, well.

MAKES 8 SERVINGS

1 tablespoon high-heat oil, such as canola or safflower

1 medium yellow onion, chopped

2 large orange or yellow bell peppers, chopped

3 medium cloves garlic, minced

1 tablespoon ground cumin

1 teaspoon ground coriander

1 teaspoon dried oregano

½ teaspoon cayenne pepper

Kosher salt and freshly ground black pepper

1½ cups cooked great northern beans, divided

1½ cups cooked navy beans

1 pound cooked turkey, shredded

1 (4-ounce) can mild diced green chilies, drained

1 (28-ounce) can tomatillos, drained and roughly chopped

4 cups chicken stock

Crumbled cotija cheese or sour cream, for serving

Lime wedges, for serving

In a large pot over medium heat, heat the oil. Add the onion and peppers and cook, stirring often, until the onion is translucent and the peppers are softened, 5 to 7 minutes. Add the garlic, cumin, coriander, oregano, cayenne, salt, and black pepper to taste; cook until fragrant, about 2 minutes.

(CONTINUED)

In a small bowl, mash ½ cup of the great northern beans.

Add the mashed beans, remaining 1 cup great northern beans, navy beans, turkey, chilies, tomatillos, and stock to the pot; stir. Bring to a boil. Reduce the heat to a simmer, partially cover, and cook until the flavors meld, about 30 minutes. Season to taste with salt and pepper.

Serve topped with a handful of cheese and lime wedges for squeezing. Though crumbled cotija is the best, any shredded cheese you have in the fridge (think cheddar or Colby jack) will taste great on top.

Swap it out: Don't have turkey? Substitute cooked, shredded chicken.

Tomatill-whatos?

Sometimes called "husk tomatoes," these little green papery husk–wrapped fruits are widely used in Mexican cooking. Though not actually tomatoes (despite the literal translation from Spanish to "little tomatoes"), they are like a hip cousin, with a more sour and tangy edge. You can use them fresh (simply peel off the husks, give a quick rinse, and chop like you would a tomato) or buy them canned (where all the work is done for you).

Ash Reshteh Ⓥ
(Persian Noodle Soup)

If you're looking to clean out the cupboard and the garden simultaneously, and have an awesome meal to boot, then this is the soup for you. Four different legumes, four different herbs, and I haven't even mentioned the veggies and spices (oh, wait, I just did). One would think that with this many beans and herbs, the soup would be heavy and dense. Nothing is further from the truth! Even though it is a full meal on its own, the soup is light, refreshing, and has a surprisingly bright ending with a splash of lemon juice and all of that herby goodness.

Traditionally, this soup, served around the Persian New Year, is made with a special type of noodle and yogurt. However, we're cheating a bit and using plain ol' boxed linguine and a dollop of Greek yogurt. If you're looking to go gluten-free (per the request of my mom), see the recipe note to swap out the noodles with rice.

MAKES 6 TO 8 SERVINGS

2 tablespoons high-heat oil, such as canola or safflower

2 large yellow onions, thinly sliced

4 medium cloves garlic, minced

1 teaspoon ground turmeric

Kosher salt

1½ cups cooked chickpeas

1½ cups cooked pinto beans

1½ cups cooked kidney beans

¼ cup dried brown lentils

6 cups vegetable stock

4 ounces dried linguine, broken into 2-inch lengths

1 cup packed fresh baby spinach

1 cup chopped fresh parsley

½ cup chopped fresh chives

¼ cup chopped fresh mint

¼ cup chopped fresh dill

2 to 3 tablespoons freshly squeezed lemon juice

Freshly ground black pepper

Greek yogurt, for serving (optional)

(CONTINUED)

In a large stockpot over medium heat, heat the oil. Add the onions, reduce the heat to medium low, and cook until golden brown and almost melted (caramelized), stirring often, about 25 minutes. Stir in the garlic, turmeric, and salt to taste; cook until fragrant, about 2 minutes.

Add the chickpeas, pinto beans, kidney beans, and lentils. Pour in the stock and bring to a boil. Reduce the heat to a simmer, partially cover, and cook until the lentils are al dente, about 10 minutes.

Add the linguine, cover, and cook until the pasta is al dente and the lentils are tender, about 12 minutes. Stir in the spinach, parsley, chives, mint, and dill and stir to wilt. Season to taste with lemon juice, salt, and pepper.

Divide between bowls and top with a dollop of yogurt.

Go gluten-free: Instead of using noodles, add ½ cup rinsed and drained basmati rice along with the lentils, and a splash more stock. Bring to a boil, reduce the heat to a simmer, and cook, partially covered, until the lentils and rice are tender, about 20 minutes.

Split Pea Soup
with Bacon, Lemon, and Fresh Herbs

This is the epitome of cozy. Warm and filling, zingy with a little bit of lemon and herbs, and of course, bacon. I like eating this wrapped up in a blanket, sitting in front of a roaring fire while looking outside at the freshly fallen snow. Who am I kidding? I'm happy if I can wolf down a bowl with a grilled cheese sandwich while standing at the kitchen counter, trying to feed the kids and get them to appointments on time. Either way you serve it, it's great the day it's made but even better if it has a chance to meld flavors in the fridge overnight.

MAKES 4 TO 6 SERVINGS

½ pound bacon, finely chopped
1 medium red onion, finely chopped
3 medium ribs celery, finely chopped
2 large carrots, finely chopped
3 medium cloves garlic, minced
2 bay leaves
2 teaspoons chopped fresh thyme

2 teaspoons chopped fresh marjoram or oregano
Kosher salt and freshly ground black pepper
1 cup green or yellow split peas
4 to 5 cups chicken stock
Finely grated zest of 1 medium lemon
1 tablespoon chopped fresh chives

In a large, heavy-bottomed soup pot or Dutch oven, cook the bacon over medium-low heat, stirring occasionally, until the bacon renders its fat and begins to crisp, about 7 minutes. Add the onion, celery, carrots, and garlic. Cook until the vegetables are softened, 5 to 7 minutes. Add the bay leaves, thyme, and marjoram; season to taste with salt and pepper.

Add the split peas and coat with the bacon fat. Pour in 4 cups of the stock and bring to a boil. Reduce the heat to a simmer, partially cover, and cook until the split peas are soft, 45 to 50 minutes. Add more stock as needed.

(CONTINUED)

Remove the pot from the heat and remove the bay leaves. Stir in the lemon zest and season to taste with additional salt and pepper. Using an immersion blender, puree some of the soup to your desired preference on the scale of somewhat chunky to completely smooth (alternatively, let the soup cool for about 5 minutes and carefully transfer some of the soup in batches to the bowl of a food processor or blender). Stir in the chives.

Make it vegan: Omit the bacon and use 2 tablespoons high-heat oil, such as canola or safflower. Add a bit of liquid smoke, smoked salt, or smoked paprika. Swap out the chicken stock for vegetable stock.

Note: To make it in a slow cooker, first cook the bacon in a sauté pan over medium-low heat until the fat is rendered. Transfer to the bowl of a 6-quart slow cooker along with the vegetables, herbs, split peas, and stock. Cook on low for about 8 hours, until the split peas are tender. Add the lemon zest, chives, and salt and pepper to taste.

Ribollita
(Tuscan Bread Soup)

Let's learn how to ace the base, shall we? This dish starts with something called a *soffrito* (or *battuto* or mirepoix). It is basically a supersavory mix of aromatics (onions, celery, carrots, garlic, and herbs, to name a few), cooked low and slow to infuse a dish with flavor. It is widely used in Italian, French, Spanish, Portuguese, and Caribbean cooking, with endless variations depending on whose grandmother's recipe you use. The key is to chop everything very fine (go ahead, use a food processor if you like!) and cook it slowly. Then add it to any number of soups, stews, casseroles, rice dishes . . . anything that you want to add the je ne sais quoi element to.

MAKES 6 SERVINGS

3 cups cooked cannellini beans, divided

4 cups chicken or vegetable stock, divided

¼ cup extra-virgin olive oil, plus more for drizzling

1 large yellow onion, minced

1 large carrot, minced

2 medium ribs celery, minced

1 medium fennel bulb (about 8 ounces), minced

2 medium cloves garlic, minced

Kosher salt and freshly ground black pepper

Pinch of red pepper flakes

1 (14-ounce) can diced tomatoes

1 bunch lacinato kale (about ½ pound), tough stems removed and leaves thickly sliced

½ small (about ½ pound) green or Savoy cabbage, leaves thickly sliced

¼ cup chopped fresh parsley

¼ to ½ pound stale country bread, sliced

½ cup (about 1½ ounces) grated Parmesan cheese

(CONTINUED)

Preheat the oven to 500 degrees F.

In the bowl of a food processor or blender, puree 1 cup of the beans and 1 cup of the stock until smooth. Set aside.

In a large Dutch oven or other oven-safe casserole over medium heat, heat the oil. Add the onion, carrot, celery, fennel, and garlic and cook until a deep golden color, stirring frequently, about 15 minutes. Season to taste with salt, black pepper, and red pepper flakes.

Add the tomatoes, remaining 2 cups whole beans, pureed beans, and remaining 3 cups stock. Bring to a boil and reduce the heat to a simmer. Cook, partially covered, stirring occasionally, until the flavors meld, about 20 minutes.

Stir in the kale, cabbage, and parsley and cook until wilted and tender, 5 to 10 minutes. Lay the bread slices on top of the soup, drizzle with 1 to 2 tablespoons oil, and sprinkle with the cheese.

Transfer the dish to the oven and bake until the bread is crisp and the cheese is brown, 10 to 15 minutes. Divide between six bowls and serve immediately.

Red Lentil and Apricot Stew

This is a dish my mom has been making for years. It has that uncanny balance of sweet (hello, apricots!) and savory (hello, aromatics!). The real kicker is the surprise garlicky yogurt dolloped on top before serving. It is cooling, refreshing, and packs a punch.

MAKES 6 SERVINGS

For the yogurt sauce:
1 cup full-fat plain Greek yogurt
1 medium clove garlic, minced
2 teaspoons extra-virgin olive oil
Kosher salt and freshly ground
   black pepper

For the stew:
3 tablespoons extra-virgin olive oil
1 large yellow onion, finely chopped
4 medium cloves garlic, minced
½ cup dried apricots, finely chopped
   (psst . . . California are more flavorful
   than Turkish)

1 teaspoon ground cumin
1 teaspoon dried thyme
½ teaspoon ground turmeric (optional)
1½ cups dried red lentils
1 (14-ounce) can fire-roasted diced
   tomatoes
5 to 6 cups vegetable stock
Freshly squeezed juice of 1 medium lemon
Kosher salt and freshly ground
   black pepper
Cayenne pepper
Fresh parsley leaves, for serving

To make the yogurt sauce, in a small bowl, combine the yogurt, garlic, oil, and salt and pepper to taste. Set aside.

To make the stew, in a large, heavy-bottomed stockpot or Dutch oven over medium heat, heat the oil. Add the onion, garlic, and apricots and cook until the onion is softened, 5 to 7 minutes. Stir in the cumin, thyme, and turmeric; cook until fragrant, about 2 minutes.

Add the lentils, tomatoes, and stock. Bring to a boil. Reduce the heat to a simmer, partially cover, and cook until the lentils are tender, about 30 minutes, stirring occasionally. Season to taste with lemon juice, salt, black pepper, and cayenne pepper.

Ladle the soup into bowls and dollop with the yogurt sauce. Sprinkle with parsley leaves and serve immediately.

Sides + Salads

RECIPES TO START YOUR MEAL

———

Those dishes that start my meals often become my meals. I think it's related to my noshing gene? Sometimes I would rather sit down and eat a bunch of snacks, sides, and salads as my dinner than sit down to an actual dinner itself. I'm not entirely sure why I do this. Maybe I feel like I'm eating less? (Not true, considering the amount of sides I can eat in one sitting.) Maybe I feel like I'm eating healthier? (That's debatable, depending on how much extra cheese I pile on top.) But I'm definitely eating happier. . . . The more little sides and salads I make, the more dishes I get to try and enjoy all at once! But, of course, most of the time it happens totally unintentionally. I start noshing on a side and before I know it . . . bam. It's gone and I'm full.

I might be wrong (though I'm really never wrong. . . . Ask my husband), but I think that most people tend to think of dishes incorporating beans as "heavy." Nothing is further from the truth. Yes, it's true that I've gifted you some dishes laden with beans, cream, and cheese (and they are divine!). But bean side dishes can also be light and refreshing. And since life is all about balance, you should try them all.

HOW TO: AQUAFABA

No, it's not the newest fantastic aquatic superhero to hit the screens. Aquafaba is an ingenious way to turn something we normally throw down the drain (the liquid from canned chickpeas) into a tasty and useful subproduct. The wastewater, if you will, is actually chock-full of starches, proteins, and soluble plant solids (yum!), and makes a great vegan egg substitute. Used as is, it can be turned into an alternative egg binder in cookies and mayonnaise (see Aquafaba Mayonnaise, page 94); whipped into semistiff peaks (with a pinch of cream of tartar), it can be used to leaven waffles or muffins or as an egg white substitute; whipped into stiff peaks with a generous pinch of sugar, it can become meringue.

Though you can absolutely use the water left over from cooking your own beans, it can be a bit on the thin side and may require additional evaporation (through continued cooking). For a sure thing, use the liquid from canned chickpeas. A good rule of thumb for substitutions is 1 tablespoon aquafaba for 1 yolk, 2 tablespoons for 1 white, and 3 tablespoons for a whole egg. And yes, technically you can use any liquid from any bean. But let's just say the results will be less than appetizing in both flavor and appearance. So stick to canned chickpeas or move on.

How do you collect this magical elixir? It's as simple as draining your chickpeas in a fine-mesh sieve and collecting the runoff in a bowl. Before measuring or using the aquafaba for your recipe, make sure you give it a good shake (very James Bond, by the way . . . shaken, not stirred) to redistribute the starches.

Aquafaba Mayonnaise ⓥ

Forget the eggs and remember to keep the liquid from your can of chickpeas for this vegan version of a classic spread. One can of chickpeas will give you plenty of aquafaba to whip up a single batch of mayo—you can keep the remaining liquid in your fridge for up to one week, freeze it for later, or toss it down the drain like you probably did in the past.

MAKES 1 TO 2 CUPS

½ cup aquafaba (canned chickpea liquid)

2 teaspoons Dijon mustard

2 teaspoons apple cider vinegar

2 medium cloves garlic, minced (optional)

Granulated sugar

½ to ¾ cup neutral oil, such as canola or safflower

Kosher salt

In a tall jar, add the aquafaba, mustard, vinegar, garlic, and sugar to taste, and use an immersion blender to blend on high until frothy, about 30 seconds (alternatively, use a food processor or blender).

Slowly, over 1 to 2 minutes, stream in the oil while blending on the highest speed. The more oil you add, the denser and creamier your mayo will turn out. If using an immersion blender, gently move it up and down toward the end of mixing to incorporate a little bit of air. Season to taste with salt, and adjust mustard, vinegar, or sugar to your liking.

The mayo will thicken once cooled, so make it ahead of time and pop it in the fridge for at least 4 hours. Refrigerate any leftovers for up to 2 weeks.

Dried Cherry Pilaf ⓥ
with Chickpeas and Pistachios

I know you're not supposed to ever pick a favorite, but let's just say this dish is at the top of the list. It is sweet, savory, aromatic, and super pretty to look at. Plus, I love any excuse to use saffron in a dish. The tiny crocus stigmas (*flower threads* for the less nerdy crowd) are somewhere between sweet and savory and can be used in both desserts and main dishes. These threads cast a golden-orange hue to whatever you use them in, and a little goes a long way.

If you're extra hungry or want to turn this into a main dish instead of a side dish, add some chopped salami, chorizo, or tempeh to the pan when you cook up the shallots.

MAKES 4 TO 6 SERVINGS

2 tablespoons extra-virgin olive oil or unsalted butter
2 cups (3 to 4 large) sliced shallots
1¾ cups vegetable stock
½ cup chopped tart dried cherries
⅛ teaspoon saffron threads
Pinch of ground cinnamon

1 cup dried couscous
Kosher salt and freshly ground black pepper
1½ cups cooked chickpeas
2 tablespoons chopped fresh mint
½ cup toasted pistachios, roughly chopped (see page 38)

In a medium saucepan over medium heat, heat the oil. Add the shallots and cook until golden brown, 7 to 9 minutes.

Add the stock, cherries, saffron, and cinnamon to the saucepan. Bring to a boil. Stir in the couscous, cover, and remove from the heat. Let stand until the liquid is absorbed, about 15 minutes. Fluff with a fork and season to taste with salt and pepper.

Transfer to a serving dish and stir in the chickpeas and mint. Top with the pistachios.

Swap it out: In a pinch? If you don't want to throw down a few bucks on saffron threads, substitute ¼ teaspoon ground turmeric, paprika, or a pinch or two of ground cardamom.

Roasted Beet and Green Lentil Salad
with Orange Vinaigrette

<hr />

Whenever I eat this salad, I like to imagine myself sitting on a patio in the French countryside, sipping a glass of wine, watching the view. Truth? I've never been to France. Reality? I spent many years in a small town outside of Walla Walla, Washington, where I was a goat milker, cheese maker, and market girl. We spent a lot of time sitting on the patio in the Eastern Washington countryside, sipping glasses of wine, and watching the view. Bonus: the co-owner of the farm is French, and we had many French interns and friends visit, so I feel fairly confident that my daydreams hold water.

This is also where I fell in love with goat milk. Perhaps it was pure saturation: I spent fourteen hours a day either milking animals, making cheese, selling cheese, teaching cheese-making classes, or thinking about cheese. Or maybe it was because there is nothing quite like truly fresh chèvre eaten straight from the source. So come on a journey with me and enjoy smooth, slightly tangy goat-milk cheese sprinkled over earthy beets and lentils, with a pop of fresh herbs.

MAKES 6 SERVINGS

2 pounds golden beets

5 tablespoons freshly squeezed orange juice (from 1 to 2 medium oranges)

2 tablespoons champagne or white wine vinegar

2 tablespoons Dijon mustard

2 teaspoons finely grated orange zest (from 1 orange)

¼ cup extra-virgin olive oil

2 teaspoons chopped fresh chives

1 teaspoon chopped fresh tarragon

Kosher salt and freshly ground black pepper

2 cups cooked green lentils

4 cups arugula

4 ounces fresh goat cheese, crumbled

Preheat the oven to 450 degrees F.

Scrub the beets. Wrap the beets in foil and roast until tender, 45 to 90 minutes, depending on their size. When they are cool enough to handle, slip off the skins. Cut the beets into wedges.

In a small bowl, combine the orange juice, vinegar, mustard, and orange zest. Slowly drizzle in the oil while whisking to create an emulsified vinaigrette. Stir in the chives and tarragon. Season to taste with salt and pepper.

In a large bowl or serving platter, combine the beets, lentils, arugula, and dressing. Sprinkle with the cheese and serve warm or chilled.

Swap it out: Use brown lentils instead of green.

Got Greens?
If your beets come with the leaves attached, tear the greens into bite-size pieces. Toss them with a little oil and roast at 450 degrees F on a baking sheet for about 5 minutes, until just crisp. Sprinkle on top of the salad before serving.

Slow Cooker Molasses Baked Beans

Along with traditional navy beans, these baked beans use great northern and cannellini. You can really use any remnants of dried beans you may have floating in your cupboard, as long as they have about the same cooking time (check the Bean-cyclopedia on page 151, if you're not sure). The final dish is everything you could ask for in a baked bean dish: smoky, sweet, thick, tangy, and a touch sticky.

Speaking of sweet . . . it's important to wait until the beans are almost tender before adding the sugar and molasses. In addition to being sweet, molasses has an acidic component to it, and both the sugar and acid can prevent the beans from ever getting really tender if you add it too soon. All good things come to those who wait. Don't rush it.

MAKES 8 TO 10 SERVINGS

⅔ cup dried navy beans

⅔ cup dried great northern beans

⅔ cup dried cannellini beans

3 ounces (about 6 strips) bacon, chopped, or 2 teaspoons high-heat oil, such as canola or safflower

1 large yellow onion, diced

4 medium cloves garlic, minced

3 cups chicken or vegetable stock

3 tablespoons Dijon mustard

1 tablespoon Worcestershire sauce

2 teaspoons chili powder

½ cup dark brown sugar

¼ cup molasses

Kosher salt and freshly ground black pepper

1 to 2 tablespoons apple cider vinegar

In a large bowl, cover the beans with 2 to 3 inches of cold water and soak using the quick or long method described on page 19 (bonus points if you brine the beans; see page 20). Drain and rinse.

If you are using bacon, heat a medium sauté pan over medium-high heat. Add the bacon and let the fat render, about 5 minutes. Add the onion and cook until the bacon is crisp, 7 to 10 minutes. If not using bacon, in a medium sauté pan over medium-high heat, heat the oil. Add the onion, and cook until translucent and soft, about 7 minutes. Stir in the garlic and cook until fragrant, about 2 minutes.

In a 6-quart slow cooker, combine the onion mixture, beans, stock, mustard, Worcestershire sauce, and chili powder. Cover and cook on low until the beans are just tender, 6 to 7 hours.

Remove the lid and stir in the brown sugar, molasses, and salt and pepper to taste. Let simmer, partially covered, for 30 minutes to 1 hour to let the flavors meld and the sauce thicken.

Before serving, season to taste with vinegar and additional salt and pepper, if needed.

Swap it out: Don't have a slow cooker? Follow the recipe above, except finish the cooking process in a Dutch oven or other oven-safe casserole at 325 degrees F for 4 to 5 hours, stirring occasionally. Add the sugar, molasses, salt, and pepper once the beans are cooked through, return it to the oven, and let simmer for an additional 30 minutes to meld the flavors.

Note: To avoid stickiness, spray your measuring cup with a little oil before measuring the molasses. This works for honey too.

A Bit of Booze
If you like the hard stuff, add about ¼ cup of your favorite bourbon with the molasses and brown sugar.

Cauliflower and Lima Bean Gratin

The first gratin I ever encountered was in culinary school. My school adhered to the more traditional French style of cooking, so we made dishes with a lot of heavy cream, cheese, and carbs (I've got no problem with that). I remember falling in love with the concept of this dish: thinly sliced veggies baked to tender perfection in delicious, creamy, cheesy goodness. Often in a pretty dish with a golden crust and fresh herbs sprinkled on top. Nope, no problem at all.

I like to add just a touch of heat to my gratins, whether in the form of horseradish, red pepper flakes, or hot sauce. I think it adds a nice balance to the richness of the dish. Life is all about balance, after all. Speaking of which, because this dish is so rich, consider serving it alongside a fresh green salad or baked chicken or fish so you don't instantaneously fall into a deep, dreamy food coma.

MAKES 6 TO 8 SERVINGS

3 tablespoons unsalted butter, plus more for the dish

1 cup (about 2 large) sliced shallots

4 medium cloves garlic, minced

3 tablespoons all-purpose flour

2½ cups whole milk

1½ cups (about 6 ounces) grated Gruyère cheese

1 to 2 tablespoons prepared horseradish

½ cup chopped fresh parsley, divided

Kosher salt and freshly ground black pepper

1 (2- to 3-pound) head cauliflower, cut into ¼-inch-thick slices

3 cups cooked lima beans

1 cup fresh bread crumbs

½ cup (about 1½ ounces) grated Parmesan cheese

1 cup lightly toasted whole walnuts, chopped (see page 38)

(CONTINUED)

Preheat the oven to 350 degrees F. Lightly butter a 3-quart (9-by-13-inch) baking dish.

In a large saucepan over medium heat, melt the butter. Add the shallots and garlic and cook until softened, about 5 minutes. Sprinkle the flour over the top and incorporate, stirring until fully combined, 2 to 3 minutes. Slowly whisk in the milk (really, y'all! Really slowly), a little at a time to create a thick, creamy sauce. Let simmer until thickened, about 5 minutes, stirring occasionally.

Remove from the heat and whisk in the Gruyère cheese, horseradish, and ¼ cup of the parsley. Season to taste with salt and pepper.

Combine the cauliflower and beans in the baking dish. Pour the sauce over the vegetables and jiggle the pan to settle the sauce.

In a small bowl, combine the bread crumbs, Parmesan cheese, walnuts, and remaining ¼ cup parsley. Sprinkle over the top of the casserole.

Bake for 40 to 50 minutes, until the cauliflower is just tender and the top is golden brown. Let cool for 20 minutes before serving.

Swap it out: Don't like lima beans? Try navy or great northern beans.

Cannellini and Kale Salad Ⓥ
with *Tahini Dressing*

We often cook kale because it's a hardy green that can withstand a bit of heat and still maintain a semblance of texture. However, that hardiness can be a tad indigestible when eaten raw. It may sound odd, but massaging the raw leaves with oil helps to break down the tough cell structure, leaving the leaves more gentle in both taste and consistency. To start the process, remove the stems from the leaves (you can use a knife but it's much quicker to simply run your fingers on either side of the stem and peel the greens away). Slice your greens, toss them in some oil, and practice your best massage technique. And, like any good bodywork, it's always advisable to listen to your client—work the kale enough that it's relaxed with a bit of bite, but not so much that it turns into a pile of mush.

I like to think of this salad as an alternative Caesar—a bit healthier, a bit more vegetarian, a bit more hip.

MAKES 4 SERVINGS

1½ cups (2 to 3 ounces) cubed country bread
2 tablespoons extra-virgin olive oil, divided
2 medium cloves garlic, minced, divided
Kosher salt and freshly ground black pepper
1 bunch lacinato kale (about ½ pound), tough stems removed and leaves sliced into ½-inch ribbons

3 tablespoons freshly squeezed lemon juice, divided
2 tablespoons tahini
1 tablespoon granulated sugar, to taste
1 tablespoon chopped fresh parsley
Dash of hot sauce
1 to 2 tablespoons hot water, or as needed
1½ cups cooked cannellini beans
¼ cup (about ¾ ounce) grated Parmesan cheese (optional)

(CONTINUED)

Preheat the oven to 350 degrees F.

In a large bowl, toss the bread, 1 tablespoon of the oil, 1 clove of the garlic, and salt and pepper to taste. Spread on a baking sheet and bake until golden brown, about 15 minutes, stirring halfway through. Set aside to cool.

Place the kale in a large bowl. Toss with the remaining 1 tablespoon oil, 1 tablespoon of the lemon juice, and salt and pepper to taste. Use your hands to massage the kale until it breaks down a bit, about 3 minutes. Set aside.

In a small bowl, combine the tahini, remaining 2 tablespoons lemon juice, remaining 1 clove garlic, sugar, parsley, and hot sauce. Whisk, thinning with hot water if necessary, to get a pourable consistency. Season to taste with salt and pepper.

In a large serving dish, combine the beans, kale, and dressing. Garnish with the croutons and cheese.

Go gluten-free: Replace the croutons with ¼ cup toasted sunflower seeds (see page 38).

Swap it out: Don't want to get so cozy with your kale? Replace the larger torn leaves with a 10-ounce carton of baby kale, and no funny business.

Edamame Slaw Ⓥ

I could probably eat some version of coleslaw every day. I especially like this coleslaw twist: light, tangy, and uniquely savory (thank you, miso and sesame oil!). It's a totally different approach from those sweet and creamy side dishes that you often see piled next to sandwiches and barbecued pork. Don't get me wrong, you can absolutely serve this alongside sandwiches and barbecued pork, but maybe change it up a bit with *banh mi* or *char siu*.

Miso, a fermented paste made from soybeans, comes in three different flavors, indicated by their hue. White and yellow tend to be milder, while red has a little more punch. Which should you use for this dressing? That's up to you.

MAKES 4 SERVINGS

3 tablespoons soy sauce

2 tablespoons freshly squeezed lime juice

2 tablespoons rice or white wine vinegar

1 tablespoon miso paste (any color)

2 teaspoons minced peeled fresh ginger

1 medium clove garlic, minced

3 tablespoons toasted sesame oil

1 tablespoon sesame seeds, toasted (see page 38)

Dark brown sugar

2 cups (about 7 ounces) shredded red cabbage

2 cups (about 7 ounces) shredded green cabbage

2 cups shelled cooked edamame (see page 23)

1 cup (about 1 large) shredded carrots

½ cup (about 4) sliced green onions, both white and green parts

¼ cup roughly chopped fresh cilantro

In a small bowl, whisk the soy sauce, lime juice, vinegar, miso, ginger, and garlic. Slowly drizzle in the oil while whisking to create an emulsified vinaigrette. Stir in the sesame seeds and season to taste with sugar.

In a large bowl, combine the cabbage, edamame, carrots, green onions, and cilantro. Drizzle with the dressing and toss to combine.

Note: Instead of hand shredding cabbage and carrots, cheat just a little bit by grabbing two 8-ounce bags of coleslaw mix from the grocery store.

Warm Potato, Apple, and Lentil Salad ⓥ

I've never been a fan of the traditional potato salad: overcooked cubes of potatoes swimming in mayonnaise, chunks of eggs floating around yelling for help, perhaps a bit of green from celery or parsley, if you're lucky. This here is potato salad, elevated. Lentils add protein, apples add a crisp acidic component, and the dressing is light and bright. Not a spot of mayonnaise to be seen. Sure, you can serve this version alongside a burger, but it really deserves a prominent spot next to a perfectly cooked piece of salmon, steak, or Field Roast at your next dinner party.

MAKES 6 TO 8 SERVINGS

¼ cup Dijon mustard

¼ cup (from ½ medium) minced red onions

¼ cup apple cider vinegar

¼ cup apple juice

¼ cup extra-virgin olive oil

Kosher salt and freshly ground black pepper

2 cups cooked brown lentils, warm

4 medium ribs celery, chopped into ¼-inch pieces, plus leaves

2 medium sweet-tart apples (Honeycrisp, Braeburn, etc.), cored and chopped into ¼-inch pieces

¼ cup chopped fresh parsley

1½ pounds fingerling potatoes, chopped into ¼-inch pieces

In a small bowl, whisk the mustard, onions, vinegar, and juice. Slowly drizzle in the oil while whisking to create an emulsified vinaigrette. Season to taste with salt and pepper.

In a large bowl, combine the lentils, celery and leaves, apples, dressing, and parsley. Set aside.

Add the potatoes to a large pot with cold, heavily salted water. Bring to a boil and cook until tender but not mushy, 5 to 7 minutes. Drain well and toss with the lentil mixture while still hot. Serve immediately.

Swap it out: Green lentils are equally delicious in this recipe.

Saladu Ñebbe Ⓥ
(Senegalese Black-Eyed Pea Salad)

This is the type of salad that I end up eating half of while preparing it. There is something about all of the fresh, crisp veggies, bright lime juice, and touch of heat that I . . . Just. Can't. Stop. So, theoretically, this dish makes enough for five friends and family to enjoy as well. But it never seems to stretch that far when I make it. I've also been known to turn this into a nice little lunch by serving it over leftover cooked brown rice. Every once in a while, I'll wrap it up in a tortilla, but you should eat it alone and over a plate, because I'll be honest: it's a bit messy.

The trick to making this salad is to cut all of the vegetables the same size as the black-eyed peas. That way you get a perfect blend of every scrumptious pea-size morsel in one spoon. Or two spoons. Or again, all of the spoons while you're standing over the mixing bowl. Why can't I stop?!

MAKES 6 SERVINGS

½ cup chopped fresh parsley
¼ cup freshly squeezed lime juice
   (from 2 to 3 limes)
1 tablespoon Dijon mustard
1 teaspoon ground cumin
6 tablespoons extra-virgin olive oil
Kosher salt and freshly ground
   black pepper

3 cups cooked black-eyed peas
3 large Roma tomatoes, cored and diced
1 medium English cucumber, diced
1 large yellow or orange bell pepper, diced
1 to 2 habanero or jalapeño peppers,
   seeded and minced (optional)
4 green onions, both white and green
   parts, sliced

In a small bowl, whisk the parsley, lime juice, mustard, and cumin. Slowly drizzle in the oil while whisking to create an emulsified vinaigrette. Season to taste with salt and pepper.

In a large bowl, mix the black-eyed peas, tomatoes, cucumber, peppers, and green onions. Dress with the vinaigrette. Refrigerate for at least 4 hours, stirring occasionally, to allow the flavors to meld.

Serve cold or at room temperature.

Edamame and Green Lentil Salad
with Grapes and Feta

Strangest combination of ingredients you've ever seen, you say? Okay. I'll admit this one threw me for a loop at first too. A lean, green salad machine, this dish was inspired partly by mad-scientist experiment and partly by trying to use leftovers from the fridge. Initially, I too had a problem with lentils, edamame, and grapes cohabitating. But my mind has opened and I'm a new person willing to accept and love all types of bean intermingling. It's unexpected, it's unconventional, it's savory, it's sweet, it's tart, it's fresh . . . it kind of sounds like my marriage, actually. Maybe that's why I like it so much? Side note: Hi, babe, thinking 'bout you! Now, getting back to work.

MAKES 4 TO 6 SERVINGS

½ cup dried green lentils

1½ cups shelled raw edamame (see page 23)

¼ cup freshly squeezed lemon juice (from about 2 medium lemons)

2 tablespoons Dijon mustard

3 tablespoons extra-virgin olive oil

Kosher salt and freshly ground black pepper

1½ cups halved or quartered grapes

2 cups arugula

2 tablespoons sliced fresh mint

1 cup toasted pecans, roughly chopped (see page 38)

½ cup (about 2 ounces) crumbled feta cheese

Put the lentils in a medium saucepan and cover generously with water. Bring to a boil over high heat, cover, and reduce the heat to a simmer. Cook until the lentils are almost tender, about 20 minutes. Add the edamame and continue to cook until the lentils are fully tender, about 5 more minutes. Drain the excess water.

In a small bowl, combine the lemon juice and mustard. Slowly drizzle in the oil while whisking to create an emulsified vinaigrette. Season to taste with salt and pepper.

In a large bowl, add the lentil-edamame mixture. Toss with the dressing, grapes, arugula, mint, pecans, and cheese. Serve warm or chilled.

Suppers + Square Meals

RECIPES FOR THE MAIN TABLE

—

This is where we get to the real meat, er . . . beans, of the book. Where legumes are the centerpiece of the dish and the table. Be you vegan, vegetarian, or a *Tyrannosaurus rex*, there is a main dish (or two or three or ten) that will please your palate, fill your belly, and probably give you some great leftovers for lunch the next day.

Some of these recipes lean toward the meat-and-dairy free zone, while others are decidedly in carnivorous territory. But don't fret! Almost all of these recipes are perfectly adaptable to whatever diet you may follow. I'll be honest, I don't have vegetable stock in my house. I shop at one of those warehouse stores, so I have about one hundred thousand boxes of chicken stock. When a recipe calls for vegetable stock, do I run out to the store and buy some? Nope. I use what I have. But I also have a gluten-free mother and a vegetarian and dairy-free sister-in-law. Do I sometimes skip the bread, meat, and cheese? Heck ya. I also have a bacon-loving hubby. Might I sneak a slice or two into a vegetarian recipe? You betcha. Make these recipes work for you and yours—feel free to wiggle around a little. Like a perfect pair of jeans, you'll find them to be very forgiving.

HOW TO: FLAVOR BOOSTERS

You may notice that many of these recipes call for something a little extra added to the cooking water, whether it is stock, herbs, or a bit of meat. Yes, beans taste great cooked with just plain ol' water, but they taste even better when cooked in a liquid loaded with flavor.

If you're cooking dried beans from scratch before you add them to the main dish, you can boost your beans with a touch of flavor added to the cooking liquid. Fresh herb sprigs, tied with kitchen twine so that they are easy to remove later on, add a ton of flavor and may even help to reduce gas and increase the absorption of iron. Try rosemary, thyme, parsley, epazote, or sage. Every chef's secret ingredient, mirepoix, is an easy way to add flavor: Finely (if you plan on leaving them in) or roughly (if you plan on taking them out) chop onions, carrots, and celery and add them to the pot. A few whole peeled cloves of garlic also add a nice touch.

There's a reason the dish pork and beans is so famous. Beans love meat. Adding a ham hock, some bacon, or a marrowbone, or using chicken stock will add depth of flavor to your meal. Of course, use this option only if you are not inviting vegetarian or vegan family members or neighbors over to dinner.

Bean Bourguignonne ⓥ

It's warm, it's hearty, I might like to curl up in bed with it on a cold winter's night. It's all the classic ingredients found in a traditional beef bourguignonne, without the beef, of course. So, a not-traditional-but-somewhat-traditional dish with a bean twist. I couldn't resist throwing in a bit of bacon for some smoky, meaty flavor, but if you're going meatless (or, gasp, just don't care for bacon), the dish is still warm, hearty, and delicious without it.

MAKES 6 TO 8 SERVINGS

3 cups cooked great northern beans, divided

3 to 4 cups vegetable, mushroom, or chicken stock, divided

6 ounces bacon, chopped (optional)

1 to 3 tablespoons extra-virgin olive oil, as needed

1 large yellow onion, sliced

1 pound carrots, cut into ½-inch slices

1 pound cremini mushrooms, stems removed and caps quartered

4 medium cloves garlic, minced

2 teaspoons chopped fresh thyme, or 1 teaspoon dried thyme

2 tablespoons tomato paste

1½ cups red wine, such as syrah, cabernet sauvignon, or merlot

1½ cups cooked navy beans

2 bay leaves

Kosher salt and freshly ground black pepper

½ cup chopped fresh parsley, for serving

In the bowl of a food processor or blender, puree 1 cup of the great northern beans and 1 cup of the stock until smooth. Set aside.

Heat a large, heavy-bottomed pot over medium-high heat. Add the bacon and let the fat render, about 5 minutes. Remove the bacon with a slotted spoon and set aside.

Add 1 tablespoon of the oil and the onion, carrots, and mushrooms to the bacon fat in the pot (if making this vegan, use 3 tablespoons oil instead). Cook until the vegetables soften and start to brown, about 10 minutes. Stir in the garlic and thyme and cook until fragrant, about 2 minutes. Add the tomato paste and stir until incorporated, about 1 minute. Return the bacon to the pot.

Pour in the wine and scrape the bottom of the pot to loosen any browned bits. Bring the liquid to a simmer, and simmer until reduced by half, 5 to 10 minutes. Add the remaining 2 cups great northern beans, the pureed beans, the navy beans, bay leaves, and remaining 2 to 3 cups stock to cover, bring to a boil. Reduce the heat to a simmer, partially cover, and cook for 30 minutes to meld the flavors.

Season to taste with salt and pepper and garnish with the parsley before serving.

Lima Bean Risotto with Almonds ⓥ

Risotto was one of the first things I learned to cook in a "real" kitchen (read: not home, not culinary school, but a place where I was actually paid to cook) in my early days of catering. The fellas made me cook it the old-fashioned way: standing over the pot, constantly stirring with a wooden spoon, without respite. Yes, in reality it's okay to leave the pot once in a while (some people don't even stir at all . . . gasp!), but I prefer to stick to my roots. I make my risotto the same way every time: sauté my aromatics, toast my rice, then lovingly stir in my stock a cup at a time until the rice is perfectly al dente (just a little bit of bite or tooth). It may not technically make the dish creamier than an unattended pot, but giving it all that love and attention, just like kids and puppies, will result in a happier and more balanced dish.

MAKES 4 SERVINGS

4 tablespoons extra-virgin olive oil, divided
½ cup (about 1 large) finely chopped shallot
4 medium cloves garlic, minced, divided
1 cup arborio rice
½ cup white wine
4 to 5 cups vegetable broth, hot
2 tablespoons nutritional yeast (optional)

2 teaspoons finely grated lemon zest
1 teaspoon chopped fresh thyme
Kosher salt and freshly ground
  black pepper
1½ cups cooked lima beans
½ cup raw sliced almonds

In a large, wide saucepan over medium heat, heat 3 tablespoons of the oil. Add the shallots and sauté until translucent, about 3 minutes. Stir in 3 of the minced garlic cloves and cook until fragrant, about 2 minutes. Pour the rice into the pan and stir to coat with oil. Continue stirring until the rice edges are translucent and the rice smells fragrant and toasted, about 3 minutes. Pour in the white wine and stir to deglaze the pan (scrape up the tasty brown bits on the bottom); simmer until reduced by half, 2 to 3 minutes.

(CONTINUED)

Add 1 cup of the hot broth, stirring frequently until it is absorbed. Continue adding the broth 1 cup at a time until the rice is al dente, 15 to 20 minutes. Stir in the nutritional yeast, lemon zest, and thyme. Season to taste with salt and pepper.

In a large sauté pan over medium heat, heat the remaining 1 tablespoon olive oil. Add the beans and almonds and sauté until the almonds are toasted, 5 to 6 minutes. Stir in the remaining 1 clove garlic and cook until fragrant, about 2 minutes. Season to taste with salt and pepper.

Gently fold the lima bean mixture into the risotto. Season to taste with salt and pepper and serve immediately.

Swap it out: Got milk? If you want to add additional creaminess to the dish, swap out 1 cup of vegetable stock with milk or cream and add a healthy handful of grated Parmesan cheese in lieu of the nutritional yeast.

Coconut-Curry Split Pea Dal ⓥ

It's a chicken-and-egg situation: dal is both an ingredient and a dish. The word refers to dried split pulses (specifically lentils or split peas), but it also refers to the thick stews and soups that are made from those pulses. So which came first? We may never know, and I'm okay with that.

This dish is spicy, but not too spicy. Fragrant, but not overpowering. It is great the first day, but it is beyond fantastic the second or third day. So, if you can, make it ahead of time.

MAKES 6 SERVINGS

2 tablespoons coconut oil

2 medium yellow onions, thinly sliced

4 medium cloves garlic, minced

2 tablespoons finely chopped
   peeled fresh ginger

2 teaspoons cumin seeds

2 teaspoons fennel seeds

2 teaspoons curry powder

1 teaspoon ground turmeric

1 red chili or serrano pepper,
   seeded and sliced

1½ cups dried yellow split peas

1 (14-ounce) can full-fat coconut milk

1 (14-ounce) can diced tomatoes

3 to 4 cups vegetable stock

1 cup packed fresh baby spinach

Kosher salt and freshly ground
   black pepper

Cooked rice or naan, for serving

Lime wedges, for serving

In a large saucepan over medium-high heat, heat the oil. Add the onions and cook until softened, 5 to 7 minutes. Stir in the garlic, ginger, cumin, fennel, curry, turmeric, and chili and cook until fragrant, about 2 minutes.

Add the split peas to the pan and cook for 2 minutes, stirring constantly to coat them in the oil and spices. Pour in the coconut milk, tomatoes, and enough stock to cover by 1 to 2 inches. Bring to a boil, reduce the heat to a simmer, partially cover, and cook until the split peas are tender, stirring occasionally, 50 to 60 minutes. Stir in the spinach and cook until wilted, 2 to 3 minutes. Season to taste with salt and pepper.

Serve over rice or alongside naan, with the lime wedges.

Lima Bean Frittata
with Halloumi Cheese

My hubby didn't think he would like this because "it's just eggs" and "the ingredients sound funny." Well, I'm happy to report that he ate three servings for dinner and took the rest to work. So, what does he know?

Za'atar is a Middle Eastern spice blend. It's basically like salt, but a gazillion times better. If you can't find any locally and don't want to order it online, you can make your own (recipe follows). What do you do with the extra? Toss it on roasted veggies and meats, stir it into dips, add it to salad dressings. . . . Put it on everything!

MAKES 6 SERVINGS

6 large eggs

½ cup whole milk

¼ cup chopped fresh parsley

2 tablespoons chopped fresh mint

Kosher salt and freshly ground
   black pepper

2 tablespoons extra-virgin olive oil

2 medium yellow onions, sliced

1½ cups cooked lima beans

3 medium cloves garlic, minced

2 teaspoons za'atar, store-bought
   or homemade (recipe follows)

½ cup (about 2 ounces) grated
   Halloumi cheese

Preheat the oven to 375 degrees F.

In a large bowl, whisk the eggs until well blended and slightly frothy. Add the milk, parsley, and mint; whisk to combine. Season generously to taste with salt and pepper. Set aside.

In a 10-inch cast-iron sauté pan (or other stove-to-oven-safe pan) heat the oil over medium heat. Add the onions, reduce the heat to medium low, and cook until caramelized, stirring occasionally, about 25 minutes. Add the beans, garlic, and za'atar and cook until fragrant, about 2 minutes.

(CONTINUED)

Pour the egg mixture over the bean mixture. Let cook on the stove top, without stirring, until the eggs just begin to set, 3 to 4 minutes. Sprinkle the cheese over the top.

Transfer the pan to the oven and bake until the frittata is golden and puffed, about 15 minutes. Slice into wedges and serve.

Swap it out: Hello, Halloumi! Halloumi is a semisoft goat and sheep milk cheese that has been brined and has a high melting point. If you don't have Halloumi cheese on hand, crumbled feta cheese makes an excellent substitute.

HOMEMADE ZA'ATAR

MAKES ABOUT 6 TABLESPOONS

2 tablespoons dried oregano

1 tablespoon sesame seeds, toasted and cooled (see page 38)

1 tablespoon sumac or dried lemon zest

1 tablespoon dried thyme

1 tablespoon dried marjoram

1 teaspoon kosher salt

In a small bowl, mix the oregano, sesame seeds, sumac, thyme, marjoram, and salt. Store in a cool, dry place for 3 to 6 months.

Frijoles Negros ⓥ
(Slow Cooker Cuban Black Beans)

Most of the time we soak beans to aid in digestibility and help them cook quickly. However, for this recipe we throw the rule book at the wall. You can simply toss your unsoaked (gasp!) black beans right into the slow cooker, and after seven to eight hours they turn into a perfectly cooked, creamy, flavorful dish.

When served with rice, this dish is a meal in itself. But if you're feeding the hordes (or just having my family over for dinner), we like to add some cooked sliced sausage just before serving. Andouille if you're feeling spicy, Italian if you're feeling conservative, tofu if you're feeling vegan. If you're not feeding the hordes and have a bit left over, transfer the cooled beans to storage containers and freeze. Turn the leftovers into soup, dip, burrito filling, or, you know, just eat them with rice again!

MAKES 8 TO 10 SERVINGS

1 tablespoon high-heat oil, such as canola or safflower
1 large yellow onion, diced
1 large green bell pepper, diced
3 medium cloves garlic, minced
2 bay leaves
2 teaspoons ground cumin
2 teaspoons dried oregano
1 pound dried black beans
4 cups vegetable stock

1 (14-ounce) can full-fat coconut milk
Finely grated zest and freshly squeezed juice of 1 large lime
Kosher salt and freshly ground black pepper
Hot sauce
Cooked rice, for serving
3 tablespoons chopped fresh cilantro, for serving

(CONTINUED)

In a medium skillet over medium-high heat, heat the oil. Add the onion and cook until translucent, about 5 minutes. Stir in the pepper, garlic, bay leaves, cumin, and oregano; cook until fragrant, about 2 minutes.

Transfer the onion mixture to a 6-quart slow cooker along with the beans, stock, and coconut milk. Cover and cook on low for 7 to 8 hours, until the beans are tender.

Remove the bay leaves and discard. Measure out 2 cups of cooked beans. Transfer to a small bowl and mash. Add the mashed beans back to the slow cooker. Stir in the lime zest and juice, and season to taste with salt, pepper, and hot sauce.

Serve the beans over the rice, sprinkled with cilantro.

Swap it out: Don't have a slow cooker? Bring the ingredients to a boil in a large, heavy-bottomed pot on the stove top and partially cover. Reduce the heat to a simmer and cook until the beans are tender, about 2 hours. Finish with the lime juice, zest, salt, pepper, and hot sauce.

Black-Eyed Pea Jambalaya Ⓥ

Most of the time we associate jambalaya with a dish loaded to the breaking point with shrimp, andouille sausage, and smoked chicken. There is nothing wrong with this, but sometimes you're looking for something a tad lighter, healthier, or less complicated (physically and ethically). The vegan take on this classic dish still gives you the perfect balance of smoky, spicy, hearty, tomatoey, and comforting, just without the animals. And, better yet, it is both vegan and meat-eater approved!

MAKES 6 TO 8 SERVINGS

3 tablespoons high-heat oil, such as canola or safflower, divided

1 bunch collard greens or kale (about ½ pound), stems removed and leaves sliced

1 large yellow onion, sliced

1 large red bell pepper, sliced

1 large green bell pepper, sliced

1 jalapeño pepper, seeded and minced (optional)

3 medium ribs celery, sliced

3 medium cloves garlic, minced

1½ teaspoons smoked paprika

1½ teaspoons dried oregano

1½ teaspoons dried thyme

¼ teaspoon cayenne pepper

Kosher salt and freshly ground black pepper

1 (14-ounce) can fire-roasted tomatoes

2 bay leaves

3 cups vegetable stock

1½ cups cooked black-eyed peas or kidney beans

1 cup uncooked long-grain white rice

3 tablespoons soy sauce, plus more as needed

4 green onions, both white and green parts, sliced

(CONTINUED)

Heat a Dutch oven or large, heavy-bottomed pot over medium-high heat. Add 1 tablespoon of the oil and the greens. Cook until wilted, about 5 minutes. Remove from the pot.

Add the remaining 2 tablespoons oil to the pot. Add the onion, peppers, and celery and cook until golden, about 12 minutes. Stir in the garlic, paprika, oregano, thyme, cayenne, and salt and pepper to taste; cook until fragrant, about 2 minutes. Add the tomatoes and bay leaves.

Add the stock, black-eyed peas, rice, and soy sauce to the pot. Bring to a boil, reduce the heat to a simmer, and cook, covered, until the rice is tender and the liquid is mostly absorbed, about 20 minutes.

Fold in the greens and green onions. Season to taste with additional salt, pepper, and soy sauce.

Moroccan Chermoula Chicken
with Chickpeas

Chermoula is the pesto of Morocco—a pungent sauce made from fresh herbs and spices. It is used both as a cooking sauce and serving sauce in this dish. You can use any leftovers as a topping on grilled fish, lamb, or beef. Or toss it with roasted vegetables and mix it into grain salads. Don't bother taking the time to pick off individual cilantro and parsley leaves from the stems. With soft herbs like these, you can blend the leaves and the stems together. Do give the bunches a good rinse and dry before blending, though. You can prepare the chermoula several days ahead and keep it refrigerated.

This dish is totally filling and delicious all on its own, but if you want to really up your game, serve it alongside warm couscous or Dried Cherry Pilaf with Chickpeas and Pistachios (page 97).

MAKES 4 TO 6 SERVINGS

For the chermoula:
2 teaspoons cumin seeds
½ teaspoon coriander seeds
1 bunch fresh cilantro
1 bunch fresh parsley
3 medium cloves garlic
1 teaspoon smoked paprika
Pinch of cayenne pepper
⅓ cup extra-virgin olive oil
¼ cup freshly squeezed lemon juice (from 2 medium lemons)
Kosher salt and freshly ground black pepper

For the chicken:
4 bone-in, skin-on chicken breasts, or 6 bone-in, skin-on chicken thighs (about 1 pound)
Kosher salt and freshly ground black pepper
1 tablespoon extra-virgin olive oil
1 (14-ounce) can fire-roasted tomatoes
3 cups cooked chickpeas
½ cup pitted Kalamata olives, roughly chopped
1 teaspoon smoked paprika

To make the chermoula, in a small, dry skillet over medium heat, toast the cumin and coriander seeds, shaking the pan continuously, until just fragrant, about 2 minutes.

(CONTINUED)

In the bowl of a food processor or blender, add the seeds, cilantro, parsley, garlic, paprika, and cayenne. Pulse several times to chop. With the motor running, stream in the oil and lemon juice. Season to taste with salt and pepper. Remove the chermoula from the food processor and set aside.

Preheat the oven to 400 degrees F.

Pat the chicken dry and season to taste with salt and pepper.

In a large cast-iron or other oven-safe sauté pan over medium-high heat, heat the oil. Brown the chicken on both sides, 3 to 5 minutes per side, and set aside on a plate. Drain off any excess fat.

Add the tomatoes, chickpeas, and olives to the pan, scraping up the browned bits on the bottom of the pan. Sprinkle with the paprika. Return the chicken to the pan and top with half of the chermoula.

Roast in the oven until the chicken reaches an internal temperature of 165 degrees F or the juices run clear, 40 to 50 minutes.

Serve with the reserved chermoula.

Pinto Bean Enchiladas
with Zucchini and Spinach

This one is a winner with the younger crowd in my house. Beans, rice, and cheese stuffed into tortillas, topped with sauce and more cheese, and all gooey-warm. Plus, they like extra cheese on the side (what can I say? I've raised them right). We usually use red enchilada sauce in this recipe, but I'm also a huge fan of green (and dare I say, spicy, when the kids aren't around) enchilada sauce. . . . Give it a try!

MAKES 6 TO 8 SERVINGS

1 tablespoon high-heat oil, such as canola or safflower

1 medium yellow onion, finely chopped

1 medium (about 5 ounces) zucchini, finely chopped

3 medium cloves garlic, minced

2 teaspoons chili powder

4 cups packed fresh baby spinach

Splash of vegetable stock or water

1½ cups cooked pinto beans

1 cup cooked brown rice

2 (15-ounce) cans red enchilada sauce, divided

1½ cups shredded Mexican-blend cheese, divided

Splash of red wine vinegar (optional)

Kosher salt and freshly ground black pepper

12 (8-inch) corn tortillas, warm

Sliced green onions, both white and green parts, for serving

Mexican *crema* or sour cream, for serving

(CONTINUED)

Preheat the oven to 350 degrees F.

In a large sauté pan over medium-high heat, heat the oil. Add the onion and cook until softened, 5 to 7 minutes. Add the zucchini, garlic, and chili powder and cook until the zucchini is tender, about 3 minutes. Add the spinach and stock and cook until the spinach is wilted, about 2 minutes.

Stir in the beans, rice, and ½ cup of the enchilada sauce; heat through. Remove the pan from the heat and fold in ¼ cup of the cheese. Add a splash of vinegar, and season to taste with salt and pepper.

Coat the bottom of a 13-by-9-inch baking dish with enchilada sauce.

Lay a tortilla on a work surface and add a heaping ¼ cup of the bean mixture in a line down the center. Roll up and place seam-side down in the baking dish. Continue with the remaining tortillas and bean mixture. Top with the remaining enchilada sauce and cheese.

Bake until the sauce is bubbly and the cheese is golden, 20 to 25 minutes. Top with green onions and *crema* to serve.

Swap it out: Try black beans as an alternative to pinto.

Thai Peanut Soba Salad
with Edamame and Pan-Seared Salmon

I love this dish. It can be served hot or cold. It can be served in the winter or summer. It's simultaneously light and refreshing, and hearty and comforting. It's a lean, green, veggie-and-salmon machine. But you know what I *really* like best about it? I can pull it together in less than thirty minutes with a screaming toddler underfoot. And if that doesn't speak volumes, I'm not sure what else does.

MAKES 4 SERVINGS

1 cup creamy peanut butter
¼ cup hot water
6 tablespoons soy sauce
5 tablespoons toasted sesame oil, divided
2 tablespoons freshly squeezed lime juice
4 teaspoons granulated sugar
1 teaspoon minced peeled fresh ginger
1 medium clove garlic, minced
Pinch of red pepper flakes

6 ounces soba noodles
4 (4-ounce) skin-on salmon fillets
2 cups shelled cooked edamame (see page 23)
4 cups packed fresh baby spinach or kale, roughly chopped
½ cup (about 4) sliced green onions, both white and green parts
¼ cup roasted salted peanuts, for serving

(CONTINUED)

In a small bowl, whisk the peanut butter, water, soy sauce, 4 tablespoons of the oil, lime juice, sugar, ginger, garlic, and pepper flakes. Set aside.

Cook the soba noodles according to the package directions, until just al dente, 5 to 7 minutes. Drain in a colander, and rinse under cool water if serving cold.

In a large skillet over medium-high heat, heat the remaining 1 tablespoon oil. Add the salmon and sear, flesh side down, until halfway cooked through, about 4 minutes. Carefully flip the salmon and sear, skin side down, until the desired doneness is reached and the flesh is firm to the touch, 3 to 5 minutes. Spoon 1 tablespoon peanut sauce on top of each fillet.

In a large bowl, toss the noodles, edamame, spinach, green onions, and peanut sauce to taste. Divide between four plates and top with a salmon fillet. Serve garnished with the peanuts.

Portobello Sandwiches ⓥ
with Herbed Navy Bean Spread

Some might call this a "hamburger," but since there is no meat in the "patty," I get a lot of flak from my family when I give it that title. Instead, I'll call it a sandwich. However, there is no reason you can't call it whatever you want and serve it on a hamburger bun at your next cookout when you need a vegetarian or vegan option. Just don't tell my family.

The navy bean spread, which is chock-full of fried fresh herbs and garlic, is fantastic on the mushrooms, but it also makes a wonderful dip on its own with veggies or crackers. So, if you have more than you need for your sandwiches, simply refrigerate the dip in an airtight container for up to five days.

MAKES 4 SERVINGS

For the mushrooms:
4 (5- to 6-inch diameter) portobello
   mushrooms, stems removed
3 tablespoons extra-virgin olive oil
3 tablespoons balsamic vinegar
2 medium cloves garlic, minced

For the navy bean spread:
¼ cup extra-virgin olive oil
3 medium cloves garlic, minced
1½ teaspoons chopped fresh sage
1½ teaspoons chopped fresh rosemary

1½ teaspoons chopped fresh thyme
1½ cups cooked navy beans
Drizzle of balsamic vinegar
1 to 2 tablespoons water
Kosher salt and freshly ground
   black pepper

For the sandwiches:
4 ciabatta buns
8 slices jarred roasted red bell peppers
2 cups arugula or mixed baby greens

To make the mushrooms, scrape out the gills using a spoon and discard. In a sealable plastic bag, combine the oil, vinegar, garlic, and mushrooms. Marinate at room temperature, turning occasionally, for 30 minutes.

To make the navy bean spread, in a medium sauté pan over medium-high heat, heat the oil. Add the garlic, sage, rosemary, and thyme, and cook until fragrant, about 2 minutes. Add the beans and toss to coat.

Transfer the bean mixture to the bowl of a food processor or blender and add a drizzle of balsamic vinegar. Puree until smooth, adding 1 to 2 tablespoons of water if needed. Alternatively, mash with a fork or potato masher. Season to taste with salt and pepper.

Preheat a grill to medium-high heat or heat a large cast-iron sauté pan over medium-high heat.

Grill or sear the mushrooms, turning once, until soft, 5 to 6 minutes per side. Lightly toast the buns, 1 to 2 minutes per side.

To make the sandwiches, spread both sides of the buns with the bean mixture. Place a mushroom on top of each bottom bun. Add 2 slices of the peppers and a handful of greens per sandwich. Top with the other bun halves.

Swap it out: Great northern or cannellini beans are a good alternative if you don't have navy beans.

The Best Balsamic

I used to think there was no difference in using cheap versus expensive balsamic vinegar. Once I tried the "good stuff" (aged several years and a high price tag on the supermarket shelf reflecting that), I've never been able to go back. So do yourself a favor and reach for the better vinegar. Not only will it make a marked difference in this recipe, it will elevate your cooking in general. A splash of the thick, syrupy stuff will also help keep the white bean spread nice and thick instead of adding unnecessary liquid.

Lentil, Ricotta, and Herb Meat Loaf

with Garlic-Yogurt Sauce

I grew up thinking that meat loaf was a brick of meat, with perhaps a pinch of salt or a handful of cooked oatmeal tossed in, then baked until perfectly dense. Lo and behold, as I grew older and experienced other meat loaves, I discovered that they could be moist, light, and packed with flavorful ingredients. The key to keeping this meat loaf light and juicy is to not work it too much. Dump everything in a bowl and mix it with your hands until just combined. Now is not the time for a deep-tissue massage—keep it light!

This particular meat loaf was born out of the "kitchen sink" practice (a useful culinary skill I learned from my mom), using up a bit of leftover lentils, ricotta cheese, and herbs from the garden.

MAKES 6 SERVINGS

For the meat loaf:
1 cup ricotta cheese
1 tablespoon extra-virgin olive oil
1 large yellow onion, finely chopped
2 large carrots, finely chopped
2 medium cloves garlic, minced
1½ cups cooked brown or green lentils
1 pound 80 to 85 percent lean ground beef
   (you can also use a mix of ground beef
   and ground lamb or pork)
½ cup dried bread crumbs
2 large eggs
2 tablespoons chopped fresh parsley

2 tablespoons chopped fresh oregano
2 tablespoons Worcestershire sauce
Kosher salt and freshly ground
   black pepper

For the yogurt sauce:
½ cup Greek yogurt
2 medium cloves garlic, minced
Pinch of red pepper flakes
Kosher salt and freshly ground
   black pepper

Preheat the oven to 350 degrees F.

Place the ricotta in a piece of cheesecloth or a clean kitchen towel and squeeze to remove excess moisture. Set aside.

In a medium sauté pan over medium-high heat, heat the oil. Add the onion, carrots, and garlic. Cook until softened, 5 to 7 minutes. Remove from the heat and let cool slightly.

To make the meat loaf, in a large bowl, add the onion mixture, lentils, beef, ricotta, bread crumbs, eggs, parsley, oregano, Worcestershire, and salt and pepper to taste. Using your hands, mix until just combined. Place the mixture in a 9-by-5-inch loaf pan and gently pack.

Bake until the internal temperature reaches 165 degrees F, about 75 minutes. Remove and let cool slightly.

To make the yogurt sauce, in a small bowl, combine the yogurt, garlic, and red pepper flakes. Season to taste with salt and pepper.

Slice the meat loaf and serve topped with a generous dollop of the garlic-yogurt sauce.

Bean-cyclopedia
A Quick and Easy Reference Guide

There are thousands of varieties of beans, from the adzuki to the Yankee bean (alas, there are no beans that start with the letter z; such a tragedy for this alphabetical example). And how I wish that we could cover the use, flavor, texture, and story of every bean out there. However, time is money, so we will focus on the beans that you are most likely to find in your kitchen cupboards. If you do run into exotic or enticing beans in the aisles of your grocery store or farmers market, have fun swapping them into your favorite recipe in this book if they have similar cooking times.

Pulses vary from the itsy-bitsy beluga lentil to the impressive gigante bean. They fall into four distinct categories: dried beans, dried peas, lentils, and chickpeas.

DRIED BEANS

Black Bean

The smooth and shiny shell looks a bit like a turtle, and the cooking liquid turns a dark gray-purple, making this a fun one for the littles. They have a hearty, meaty texture and a mild, almost sweet flavor, making them great in soups, stews, sauces, and served alongside rice. Black beans hold their shape when cooked and are a popular ingredient in Latin American cuisine.

ALSO KNOWN AS: Black turtle bean, turtle bean, Spanish bean

AVAILABLE AS: Canned, dried

SOAK: Believe it or not, you don't have to! But you can, for 4 to 8 hours.

STOVE TOP: 60 minutes to 2 hours

PRESSURE COOKER: 4 to 6 minutes

SWAP: Pinto, navy beans

Black-Eyed Pea

An alternative hip-hop group from the '90s or a tasty legume? Either way, you can't really go wrong. And, if we're getting down to brass tacks, the black-eyed pea is technically a bean, not a pea. It is also known as the cowpea because of its distinctive black marking on a creamy-colored background. Its earthy, ashy, mineral-y flavor is perfect in salads, rice dishes, and stews. In several cultures (in the American South and among Ashkenazi Jews, to name a few), it's considered a sign of good fortune.

ALSO KNOWN AS: Cowpea, California buckeye, goat pea

AVAILABLE AS: Canned, dried

SOAK: Doesn't have to be soaked, but will cook faster if soaked for at least 6 hours and up to 12 hours

STOVE TOP: 60 to 75 minutes

PRESSURE COOKER: 4 to 6 minutes

SWAP: Lima beans

Cannellini Bean

A paler cousin of the red kidney bean (which is why they are sometimes called white kidney beans), cannellini are creamy, slightly nutty, and bland (in a good way). Though they have a thin skin, cannellini are the largest of the white bean group and are meatier than the navy and great northern, so don't worry about offending them. Once cooked, they retain their shape quite well and have a tender bite. Cannellini are especially popular in Italian cuisine but are delicious thrown into just about every dish, such as casseroles, braises, soups, and stews.

ALSO KNOWN AS: White kidney bean, white bean

AVAILABLE AS: Canned, dried

SOAK: At least 4 hours and up to 12 hours

STOVE TOP: Boil for 10 minutes, then simmer for 1½ to 2 hours.

PRESSURE COOKER: 6 to 9 minutes

SWAP: Great northern, navy, kidney beans

Great Northern Bean

The Goldilocks of the pulse world: larger than the navy bean, smaller than the cannellini bean, and always looking for porridge. They have a mild, nutty flavor and firm flesh that holds it shape well. Great northern beans absorb the flavors of whatever you cook them with and are popular in soups and stews.

ALSO KNOWN AS: White bean

AVAILABLE AS: Canned, dried

SOAK: 8 to 12 hours

STOVE TOP: 40 to 60 minutes

PRESSURE COOKER: 8 to 10 minutes

SWAP: Navy, cannellini beans

Kidney Bean

They look a bit like a kidney both in shape and color and have a somewhat sweet, meaty flavor and firm texture. Not the most appetizing description, is it? But put my words aside, because kidney beans are wonder beans. They are great in soups, chilis, and stews and can be baked, refried, and simmered. They also love spicy foods and rice (sounds like my kind of bean). Remember though: Kidney beans contain a toxin called phytohemagglutinin, with red kidney beans containing the highest levels. To deactivate the toxin, make sure to soak them overnight, change the water, and bring them to a boil for a full 10 minutes.

ALSO KNOWN AS: Red bean (note: this is *not* the adzuki bean)

AVAILABLE AS: Canned, dried

SOAK: 8 to 12 hours

STOVE TOP: Boil for 10 minutes, then simmer for 60 to 90 minutes.

PRESSURE COOKER: 6 to 8 minutes

SWAP: Pinto, great northern, cannellini beans

Lima Bean

Lima beans are flat and smooth and have a rich, sweet-creamy flavor and a starchy-meaty texture. These beans require a long overnight soak (no short-cuts here) and a very gentle simmer so they can keep their skins together and not collapse. Though the name may sound like a sobriquet, baby lima beans are not younger beans, but a smaller, milder-tasting variety. And butter beans? Same thing but usually a bit larger (and, also, perhaps a nicer name to try to lure all of the lima bean haters to try this surprisingly creamy, mild bean). Keep in mind that the lima bean family does naturally contain a small amount of cyanide, so lima beans always need to be cooked regardless of whether they are dried or fresh. Unless, of course, you have some guests you don't want returning. Though I usually don't get too involved in your bean selection, I will say that I lean toward the canned and dried varieties over the frozen.

ALSO KNOWN AS: Butter bean, gigante bean, baby lima bean

AVAILABLE AS: Canned, dried, fresh, frozen

SOAK: 8 to 12 hours

STOVE TOP: 60 to 80 minutes

PRESSURE COOKER: 4 to 7 minutes

SWAP: Navy, cannellini, great northern beans

Navy Bean

When I was younger, I always thought this bean was blue in color because of the name. In fact, it's a small, slightly flattened off-white bean that you often find used in baked beans, dips and spreads, and soups. The name is actually derived from the fact that it has been a staple food for the US Navy since the nineteenth century. Though fairly flavorless on their own (please forgive me, navy beans!), they absorb flavors well, so are best cooked with strong flavors like pork, tomatoes, or molasses in slow-cooked stews and soups. They tend to get creamy when cooked, making them perfect for dips or thickening soups and ragouts. The navy bean gets bonus points for having the highest fiber content of all the beans.

ALSO KNOWN AS: Pea bean, Yankee bean

AVAILABLE AS: Canned, dried

SOAK: 8 to 12 hours

STOVE TOP: 60 to 90 minutes

PRESSURE COOKER: 3 to 5 minutes

SWAP: Great northern, cannellini beans

Pinto Bean

An oval bean with beige and red speckles or splotches, *pinto* means "painted" in Spanish. Really, it kind of sounds like me after a facial. Once cooked, they turn bright pink (like me in the sun) and are often used in chili and refried beans (um, not like me in any sense, I guess). The pinto is super popular in Mexican dishes, including refried beans, rice and beans, soups, and stews.

ALSO KNOWN AS: Speckled bean, strawberry bean

AVAILABLE AS: Canned, dried

SOAK: At least 4 hours and up to 12 hours

STOVE TOP: 60 to 75 minutes

PRESSURE COOKER: 6 to 8 minutes

SWAP: Kidney, great northern, black beans

Soybean (Edamame)

Okay, okay. I snuck this one in and you caught me. We are not talking about the dried soybean, which is often used for tofu, oil, margarine, flour, and animal feed. The ubiquitous soybean is the most widely produced and consumed bean in the world. And where other beans need to be paired with a grain to form a complete protein, this rock star has all the amino acids present on its own. Yes, dried soybeans can make for a tasty snack, but they're also pretty darn hard to digest and not so easy to find. So let's just gloss over this and pretend that edamame fits nicely into the dried-bean category. Deal? Deal.

Edamame is the fresh version that you often find in sushi restaurants or mixed into salads or stir-fries. Save time removing the pods (but, admittedly, losing all of the fun in eating them) by purchasing shelled beans in the freezer section.

AVAILABLE AS: Fresh or frozen

SOAK: Nope

STOVE TOP: Boil for 3 to 5 minutes.

PRESSURE COOKER: Don't even think about it.

SWAP: Snap peas, fresh beans

DRIED PEAS (WHOLE AND SPLIT)

Unlike the fresh peas you harvest in your garden and eat right then and there, dried peas are harvested and shelled once they reach full maturity. You can buy them whole (longer cooking times) or split (shorter cooking times), and they cook into a thick, creamy texture perfect for soup. The most common varieties are green and yellow split peas, which are harvested whole, then split in half. Use green or yellow split peas interchangeably in your recipes. There's no need to soak them either, though it will cut down the cooking time a bit.

SOAK: Not required

PRESSURE COOKER: 6 to 10 minutes

STOVE TOP: 30 minutes

SWAP: Green lentils

LENTILS

Like beans, lentils can be found in a variety of colors and sizes, and like peas, they can be used whole or split. They require no soaking and are the fastest cooking of all the dried legumes—usually between 20 and 40 minutes. The smaller whole lentils tend to keep their shape, and the larger flatter lentils break down quickly and have a mushier consistency. Varieties of lentils, a staple found around the world, number in the dozens, so we'll just focus on the most readily available. And here's my opinion: lentils simmer relatively quickly on the stove top. When you pop them in a pressure cooker, you risk ending up with a pile of mush. So please . . . don't.

Green Lentil

The showcase lentil, this tiny green-blue lentil has a rich flavor and maintains its shape after cooking, which is perfect for salads, casseroles, and stews. Green lentils have a nutty and peppery taste and a firm texture. Food nerd fact: originally grown in Le Puy-en-Velay, France, green lentils are now grown in Italy and North America.

ALSO KNOWN AS: Le Puy lentil, French green lentil

SOAK: Nope

STOVE TOP: 20 to 25 minutes

SWAP: Brown lentil

Brown Lentil

The workhorse of the lentil world, the brown lentil is what I like to think of as the "grocery store" lentil. They are the most common lentil, and you'll probably be able to find them at every store. Brown lentils have a creamy, nutty flavor and a somewhat firm texture that works well for patties, burgers, casseroles, and soups. But beware! Overcook this one and it will become a soft, mushy mess.

ALSO KNOWN AS: Lentil—yup, just lentil

SOAK: Nope

STOVE TOP: 20 to 25 minutes

SWAP: Green lentil

Yellow Lentil

Mild and sweet, these lentils break down quickly while cooking, making them ideal for soups and spreads. Yellow lentils are very popular in Indian curries and dal.

ALSO KNOWN AS: Golden lentil

SOAK: Nope

STOVE TOP: 15 to 20 minutes

SWAP: Red lentil

Red Lentil

Like yellow lentils, this mild and sweet legume also breaks down quickly and is popular in Indian cuisine. It has a dark pink-red color and cooks quickly.

ALSO KNOWN AS: Petite red lentil, petite crimson lentil

SOAK: Nope

STOVE TOP: 15 to 20 minutes

SWAP: Yellow lentil

CHICKPEAS

Not really peas, chickpeas are plump and firm legumes with a hazelnut shape and nutty flavor. Their soft, starchy-creamy texture makes chickpeas ideal for salads, spreads, dips, and curries. Once cooked, they hold their shape well. One of the oldest cultivated legumes, chickpeas are extensively used in Indian and Mediterranean cuisine, but are showing up everywhere nowadays. There are actually two types of chickpeas: the desi (smaller and darker) and the kabuli (larger and paler). The kabuli is the most widely available. Best yet? If you're using canned chickpeas, you get a bonus gift (learn about aquafaba on page 93)!

ALSO KNOWN AS: Garbanzo bean, *chana*, Bengal gram

AVAILABLE AS: Canned, dried

SOAK: 8 to 12 hours

STOVE TOP: 60 to 90 minutes

PRESSURE COOKER: 10 to 15 minutes

SWAP: Chickpeas are special; find a different recipe (but if you must: great northern, lima, cannellini beans).

Acknowledgments

The biggest thanks to my main bean, Evans Nguyen, without whom this book wouldn't have been possible. You were my sounding board, child wrangler, tasting panel, emotional encouragement, and tough love. You ate more beans than you ever thought possible, and dare I say, you might have even enjoyed it? Next time, I promise . . . a book on bacon.

To my boys and kitchen monkeys, Jack and Cole, who gave unapologetically honest feedback (thumbs up, down, and sideways) to almost every recipe, whether you tasted it or not. Mom and Dad, my first recipe testers (remember that pesto I made with three *heads* of garlic when I was twelve?!), I hope you enjoyed my dishes a lot more this time around. Jill Lightner, you're always keeping me on point, whether it's a teaspoon or a tablespoon (and thanks for the foot in the door). To my recipe testers near and far, old friends and new: it is your invaluable feedback that polished these ideas from unsoaked beans in the bag to splendid meals on the plate.

And, of course, a huge shout-out to my peeps at Sasquatch Books . . . Susan Roxborough, executive editor extraordinaire, thanks for keeping at me a year in the making and for all of the late-night emails, when we should have both been sleeping. Bridget Sweet and Kirsten Colton, unflappable production and copy editors with amazing skills and senses of humor. Photographer Angie Norwood Browne and food stylist Milana Zettel, you made these recipes jump to life with your beautiful photos and served up some great pho and company in the process.

Index

Conversions

VOLUME

UNITED STATES	METRIC	IMPERIAL
¼ tsp.	1.25 mL	
½ tsp.	2.5 mL	
1 tsp.	5 mL	
½ Tbsp.	7.5 mL	
1 Tbsp.	15 mL	
⅛ c.	30 mL	1 fl. oz.
¼ c.	60 mL	2 fl. oz.
⅓ c.	80 mL	2.5 fl. oz.
½ c.	120 mL	4 fl. oz.
1 c.	230 mL	8 fl. oz.
2 c. (1 pt.)	460 mL	16 fl. oz.
1 qt.	1 L	32 fl. oz.

LENGTH

UNITED STATES	METRIC
⅛ in.	3 mm
¼ in.	6 mm
½ in.	1.25 cm
1 in.	2.5 cm
1 ft.	30 cm

WEIGHT

AVOIRDUPOIS	METRIC
¼ oz.	7 g
½ oz.	15 g
1 oz.	30 g
2 oz.	60 g
3 oz.	90 g
4 oz.	115 g
5 oz.	150 g
6 oz.	175 g
7 oz.	200 g
8 oz. (½ lb.)	225 g
9 oz.	250 g
10 oz.	300 g
11 oz.	325 g
12 oz.	350 g
13 oz.	375 g
14 oz.	400 g
15 oz.	425 g
16 oz. (1 lb.)	450 g
1½ lb.	750 g
2 lb.	900 g
2¼ lb.	1 kg
3 lb.	1.4 kg
4 lb.	1.8 kg

TEMPERATURE

OVEN MARK	FAHRENHEIT	CELSIUS	GAS
Very cool	250–275	120–135	½–1
Cool	300	150	2
Warm	325	165	3
Moderate	350	175	4
Moderately hot	375	190	5
Fairly hot	400	200	6
Hot	425	220	7
Very hot	450	230	8
Very hot	475	245	9

For ease of use, conversions have been rounded.

About the Author

Jackie Freeman is a professional chef with over twenty years' experience in the culinary industry. Her work spans the range of testosterone-fueled restaurant kitchens, exotic (and not-so-exotic) destinations as a private chef, a borderline-hippie cheese maker and farmhand, a somewhere-between-strict-and-funny culinary instructor, a recipe developer with over nine hundred recipes under her testing belt, a quirky TV and radio personality, a detail-oriented food stylist, and a culinary writer.

More importantly, Jackie cooks every day for her growing (in both number and appetite) family while managing a freelance career, schlepping kids to and from school and activities, and finding a moment or two to go for a run. She brings her unique viewpoint of exacting recipe development skills and professional culinary experience and combines it with just being a regular mom trying to get a healthy, tasty, and somewhat-efficient meal on the table before the kids have a meltdown.

Printed in China

SASQUATCH BOOKS with colophon is a registered trademark of Penguin Random House LLC

24 23 22 21 20   9 8 7 6 5 4 3 2 1

Editor: Susan Roxborough
Production editor: Bridget Sweet
Designer: Alicia Terry
Photographer: Angie Norwood Browne
Author photo: Bell Lee
Food stylist: Milana Zettel

Library of Congress Cataloging-in-Publication Data
Names: Freeman, Jackie, author.
Title: Easy beans : simple, satisfying recipes that are good for you, your
    wallet, and the planet / Jackie Freeman.
Description: Seattle : Sasquatch Books, [2020] | Includes index.
Identifiers: LCCN 2020006188 (print) | LCCN 2020006189 (ebook) | ISBN
    9781632172921 (paperback) | ISBN 9781632172938 (ebook)
Subjects: LCSH: Cooking (Beans)
Classification: LCC TX803.B4 F74 2020 (print) | LCC TX803.B4 (ebook) |
    DDC 641.6/565--dc23
LC record available at https://lccn.loc.gov/2020006188
LC ebook record available at https://lccn.loc.gov/2020006189

ISBN: 978-1-63217-292-1

Sasquatch Books
1904 Third Avenue, Suite 710
Seattle, WA 98101

SasquatchBooks.com